WHEN MEMORY SPEAKS

WHEN MEMORY SPEAKS

REFLECTIONS ON AUTOBIOGRAPHY

JILL KER CONWAY

ALFRED A. KNOPF   NEW YORK   1998

THIS IS A BORZOI BOOK
PUBLISHED BY ALFRED A. KNOPF, INC.

www.randomhouse.com

Owing to limitations of space, acknowledgments for permission to
reprint previously published material may be found following the index.

Library of Congress Cataloging-in-Publication Data
Conway, Jill K., [date]
When memory speaks : reflections on autobiography /
Jill Ker Conway. — 1st ed.
p.   cm.
Includes bibliographical references and index.
ISBN 0-679-44593-5
1. Autobiography.
2. Autobiography—Women authors.
3. Biography as a literary form.
I. Title.
CT25.C68   1998
808'.06692—dc21   97-49452
CIP

Manufactured in the United States of America
Published March 20, 1998
Reprinted Once
Third Printing, April 1998

In memory of John

CONTENTS

WHEN MEMORY SPEAKS

CHAPTER ONE

MEMORY'S PLOTS

WHY IS AUTOBIOGRAPHY the most popular form of fiction for modern readers? Why are so many people moved to write their life stories today? And what is it about the genre that makes it appeal to readers not just in the Western world, but also in non-Western cultures, like those of Japan and India or the many cultures of Africa?

Since the 1950s literary critics have written hundreds of volumes about autobiography as a genre. The questions they ask come from literary theory. Is autobiography just another form of fiction? A bastard form of the novel or of biography? What sort of story can anyone tell about her or his life when its end is as yet unknown? Is it possible to translate the chaotic ebb and flow of experience into a narrative form with a beginning, a middle and an end? When so much of our consciousness is visual, or nonverbal, how much of it can we convey through the limited medium of words? Can anyone be both subject and object of the same sentences— the speaker and the subject spoken about? Why is this drive to engage in scrutiny of one's own life so characteristic of the West?

Another set of theoretical issues is raised by the study of gender. Given that Western language and narrative forms have been developed to record and explicate the male life, how can a woman write an autobiography when to do so requires using a language which denigrates the feminine and using a genre which celebrates the experience of the atomistic Western male hero? Can such literary and linguistic conventions possibly convey the bonding of maternity, or grant integrity to an experience marked by the traditions of Western misogyny?

If the autobiographer gazes at himself in the mirror of culture, just as the portrait painter must when working on his self-portrait, how should a woman use a mirror derived from the male experience? If the painter or writer is female, the mirror she holds up comes from a culture that assumes women's inferiority, a culture that has shaped modern women's inner consciousness through the internalized male gaze surveying the female as sex object. For the woman autobiographer the major question becomes how to see one's life whole when one has been taught to see it as expressed through family and bonds with others. How can she convey its authenticity when linguistic convention subsumes the female within the male? How can she construct the life history of someone other than a sex object whose story ends when soundly mated?

These theoretical issues are important, but they beg the question of why readers like to read autobiography, and why individuals are moved to write their life stories. Theory can help us read autobiography with more critical awareness. Gender studies can help us pay attention to when and where women autobiographers seem to have trouble with their narrative. But the answer to the question of why we like to read it, and why individuals sit down at desk or table and begin to tell their story, lies not in theory but in cultural history. It has to do with where we look when we try to understand our own lives, how we read texts and what largely unexamined cultural assumptions we bring to interpreting them.

Moreover, while the theoretical categories defining a genre may be fixed, its forms and stylistic patterns vary profoundly over time, and these variations constitute a kind of history of the way we understand the self, and what aspects of it we feel comfortable talking about.

This book is about readers and writers of autobiography, and about the history of self-narrative in modern and postmodern times. It is written with that comfortable fiction "the general reader" in mind. It should be taken as a background monologue to the enjoyable task of browsing the shelves of bookstore or library, or as a helpful companion on the long plane journey with a fistful of paperbacks, a fellow guest on the weekend at the beach, or even a guide in the hustle of the morning traffic, where many readers now listen to books on tape.

It is hard for us to imagine today the passion for fiction which led crowds to gather at the docks in New York in the 1840s, awaiting the arrival of the ship which was to deliver from London the latest installment of Dickens's *Old Curiosity Shop*, recounting the fortunes of its long-suffering heroine, Little Nell. Many eyewitness accounts describe the shouts as the ship carrying the next installment hove in sight. "Does Little Nell yet live?" the cry would go up, to be answered for many months in the affirmative from the decks of the approaching boat. We don't care quite that way about fiction today. Dickens's writing was reaching a popular audience which was newly literate and not yet sated with the devices for suspense developed by the serial writer. *The Old Curiosity Shop* was appearing many decades before Freud's analysis of the creative process and of the psychodynamics of fantasy, which made people view fiction as the projection of unconscious processes rather than the gifted writer's inspired reconstruction of reality. We are still interested in the projections of gifted writers' unconscious processes, but we are unlikely to model ourselves on their fictional characters, or to surrender disbelief for long enough to be concerned whether the heroine of some popular print series is still alive and well.

Of course many viewers do still feel that suspense about the characters in popular television series such as *General Hospital* or *Days of Our Lives*, but for readers of print the response is to refuse to surrender disbelief about fiction, and for writers of fiction, to move more and more into the mode of fantasy because realism is no longer accorded the attention it commanded in the great era of the modern novel, the nineteenth century.

So virtually the only prose narratives which are accorded the suspension of disbelief today are the autobiographers' attempts to narrate the history of a real life or the biographers' carefully documented historical reconstructions of lives in times past. Even this concession is not made by readers influenced by postmodern criticism, which calls into question the possibility of apprehending reality from a single point of view. Hence the convention in many forms of modern narrative of switching points of view, and leaving open the possibility of many endings for the story.

But we remain, as a species, embodied as single fleshly beings, and we experience life as though reality could be apprehended from the single locus which is the point from which we view the world. So, just as many of the truths of quantum mechanics confound our senses of the way the real world behaves, many of the justified postmodern criticisms of Western personal narratives as representations of reality seem to confound our way of seeing and feeling. We *want* to know how the world looks from inside another person's experience, and when that craving is met by a convincing narrative, we find it deeply satisfying.

The satisfaction comes from being allowed *inside* the experience of another person who really lived and who tells about experiences which did in fact occur. In this way the lost suspension of disbelief disappears and the reader is able to try on the experience of another, just as one would try on a dress or a suit of clothes, to see what the image in the mirror then looks like. We like to try on new identities because our own crave the confirmation of like experience, or the enlargement or transformation which can come from viewing a similar experience from a different perspective. When we read about totally disparate experience, say as Christians reading about a life lived by a believer in Islam, it is as though the set designer and the lighting specialist had provided us with a totally different scene and pattern of light and shadows to illuminate the stage on which we live our lives. When, for instance, we encounter a world of arranged marriages, we see the Western conventions of romantic love differently and begin to ask ourselves where those romantic feelings come from, since in another culture they simply do not occur.

Whether we are aware of it or not, our culture gives us an inner script by which we live our lives. The main acts for the play come from the way our world understands human development; the scenes and key characters come from our families and socialization, which provide the pattern for investing others with emotional significance; and the dynamics of the script come from what our world defines as success or achievement. So the inevitable happy ending of the Hollywood movie makes us feel guilty if we find ourselves unhappy or unsuccessful in life's enterprises. The Western tradition of romance makes people believe that somewhere there really is the life partner who will provide the ecstatic happiness depicted in opera, drama and fiction, so Westerners tend to become easily discouraged when such transports don't appear and may begin to keep an eye out for a new partner.

If we study the history of autobiography in Western Europe and the white settler societies that are its offshoots, it soon becomes apparent that there are archetypal life scripts for men and for women which show remarkable persistence over time. For men, the overarching pattern for life comes from adaptations of the story of the epic hero in classical antiquity. Life is an odyssey, a journey through many trials and tests, which the hero must surmount alone through courage, endurance, cunning and moral strength. Eventually, unless the hero has displeased the gods through some profoundly shocking violation of taboos, he is vindicated by his successful passage through his journey of initiation and returns to claim his rightful place in the world of his birth. His achievement comes about through his own agency, and his successful rite of passage leaves him master of his fortunes, though, of course, still subject to the whims of the gods or the turning of the wheel of destiny.

So some of the shaping male narratives of Western culture adapt this classical pattern to Christianity by moving the odyssey from the external world to the inner consciousness of the narrator, and making the journey of initiation the journey of conversion, with the narrator poised between sin and damnation, or belief and salvation. St. Augustine, in his *Confessions* (c. 400), keeps the Greek hero's agency throughout hundreds of pages as he seeks to control his wayward senses, overcome the intellectual obstacles to belief in the Christian revelation and accept subordination of his will to the will of God.[1] Even in the act of surrendering his sense of agency to God's providence, Augustine stops to review the problem of how men have knowledge of God, wondering how a man may apprehend that which is beyond the recording of the senses. In the epic description of his conversion, very much like the turning point of a battle, he makes us believe that his inner struggle is of vast and world-shaping significance. His rhetoric makes us accept that his inner struggle has ramifications which reach beyond him to the boundaries of his fourth-century world, so that though the man may surrender his will to God, his life has agency to shape the world around him. Indeed, most of us, when we read

Augustine's account of his youthful sin, the theft of some ripe pears from a neighbor's orchard, and his joy in the moment, think not of the insignificance of this adolescent lark but rather of the epoch-making significance of this man's slowly developing sense of property and of sin.

In his *Confessions* (1781) Jean-Jacques Rousseau produced a new model for the male life history. His *Confessions* tell the story of the secular hero creating himself. Rousseau keeps to the Augustinian inner story of the hero's emotional life and conflicts, but his account is without St. Augustine's sense of sin and the trajectory of his life moves not toward God but toward worldly fame and success.

Rousseau plays his moral transgressions against his picture of a corrupt aristocratic society which scorns him, and which he rejects in favor of the new democratic man, of whom he declares himself to be appropriate model. He presents himself as a man of natural manners and morals, whose transgressions against aristocratic mores are not sins but merely expressions of a new view of what is important in life. Rousseau was also the first exponent in autobiography of a new definition of the human emotions, a definition which allows a man to be governed by his senses and feelings, these being seen as more human and more authentic than externally imposed laws of conduct. Nothing could be more diametrically opposed to Augustine's fear of the senses, and worry that his eyes, ears, senses of taste and smell and sexual drives may distract him from God and embroil him in the things of this world.

In Rousseau's man of sentiment and natural feeling, we have in embryonic form the modern concept of id and ego at war with one another, feeling and culture at odds, the child surrendering innocent perceptions and feelings to enter the prison of custom and culture. Thus the democratic man claims agency through refusing to accept cultural convention and by asserting that when emotions and social prescription conflict, a man must act upon his emotions. When Rousseau becomes a thief, it is not because the devil tempts him but because he hates the master who beats him wrongfully. When he is given shelter by a Catholic woman, he pretends an interest in Roman Catholicism, not out of deceitfulness but because of a natural wish to please someone who has been kind to him. In Rousseau's life plot the classical journey of epic adventure has become an emotional one, carried on in defiance of society. It is a journey nonetheless, and one in which the hero is still an atomistic individual. Rousseau tells us, "I am made unlike any I have ever met; I will even venture to say that I am like no one in the whole world."[2] The hero is still the agent of his destiny, though the forces which drive the action of his life are not the classical fates but the war of the individual against society. The dynamic of the action comes from human passion struggling to break through the confines of inherited convention.

With the focus of attention directed to this world and the life of the emotions, the stage is set for the emergence of the Napoleonic hero, who embodies the feelings of his people in the battle for political and economic freedom; the working-class rebel, who seeks to overthrow a corrupt system of production, and the Utopian socialist hero, who is able to reconcile emotional and economic freedom. Alongside these romantic types comes the self-created economic man, first given full expression by Benjamin Franklin in his *Autobiography* (1818). The successful accumulator of wealth, who makes the journey from poverty to worldly success and triumphs through the economic disciplines of thrift, industry and deferred gratification, is a figure given archetypal form in American popular culture in the writing of Horatio Alger and in the autobiographies of captains of industry like Andrew Carnegie. In the later twentieth century, such figures blend in with the culture of celebrity created by film and television, as exemplified in the autobiographies of figures like Lee Iacocca or Katharine Hepburn.

American myth and popular culture also produced a native version of the classical odyssey, in which the frontier hero battles the wilderness, fights against savage non-Western warriors and opens "virgin" territory to white settlement. The physical struggle with the forces of nature and with "uncivilized" peoples redefines the hero's journey in Western imperialist mode, a mode that takes different forms in terms of the wilderness to be conquered and the relative degree of sophistication of conqueror and conquered. Thus we have the Spanish conquistador Bernal Díaz del Castillo, a man of little learning and less sophistication, recording his astonishment and wonder at the riches and achievement of the Indian civilization he and his fellow Spanish invaders of Mexico were laying waste in an adventure of unmitigated greed carried out in the name of Christianity.[3] In similar mode we have Christopher Columbus's account of his first encounter with the New World and the Carib people he thought might be the fabled Amazons, John Smith and Pocahontas, the Jesuit narratives of New France, Captain James Cook's reflections on Australia and its aboriginal people and travel accounts of the wonders of India, to be followed by countless narratives of discovery, conquest and eventual European settlement. In these stories of conquest the Western European male, and occasionally his female counterpart, is engaged in a literal and psychological journey. He is tested by the forces of nature and by cultural conflict, and he acts as an agent of the Western concept of progress, a god as impersonal as any Greek deity, the dynamic of history which Europeans thought promised perpetual social improvement and gave them the right to "civilize" the world in their image.

By the turn of the twentieth century, a new quest for authenticity emerged in Western European culture. The new concern with authenticity was the product of multiple interactions between economic and cultural forces. The wealth created for Europeans by the economic and technological capacity to exploit distant regions fostered the world-weariness of fin de siècle decadence. The transfer of scientific skepticism to the newly developing social sciences resulted in the idea of cultural relativism. This reductive view of culture was the framework within which materialist economics combined with the first efforts to develop comparative studies of religion to define religious belief as a form of neurosis. And the visible and cultural effects of a fully articulated urban industrial production system raised for the first time the possibility of a radical break between nature and the engineered environment. Decadence, cultural relativism, lost belief and the break with nature were major themes of modernism which gave rise to a new type of autobiography, the story of the modern quest for meaning, given classic form in narratives like James Joyce's *Portrait of the Artist as a Young Man* (1916) and poetic expression in T. S. Eliot's "Ash Wednesday" (1930) and the *Four Quartets* (1942).

In the late twentieth century, after two military catastrophes in which Europeans consumed their wealth and undermined the central values of their Judeo-Christian roots, witnessed or were participants in the evil of the Holocaust and fostered the invention of atomic and biological weapons, the confident European imperialist narrative was replaced by the postmodern refusal to recognize a central point of view from which the world is to be seen. This refusal has been accompanied by an outpouring of autobiographical statements of ethnic identity, which have their most striking form in English in the writing of African-Americans like Malcolm X and James Baldwin, or in the narratives of Westernized leaders of other cultures like Jawaharlal Nehru or his Muslim counterpart, Mohammed Ali Jinnah. The same cultural forces have encouraged assertions of sexual difference, as in James Merrill's recent classic account of a homosexual coming of age.[4]

The history of women's autobiographical writing in Europe and its offshoots underlines the extent to which experience is both shaped by gendered difference and subject to the same economic and cultural forces which influence the shape and style of male narratives. To begin with, women inherited a different tradition from classical antiquity and early Christianity than the one which shaped St. Augustine's consciousness. Classical antiquity provided only the myth of the Amazons for the image of female heroic action and saw the image of the physically powerful female as monstrous rather than admirable. The fabled Greek democracies revered by the post-Renaissance West did not count women as citizens and left them out of the political theory which was central to the Western ideal of democracy and of citizenship. Although the women of the Hebrew Scriptures gave ample evidence of the power to rule, and to bear witness, the Pauline influence on the Christian Scriptures gave early Christianity its fear of the senses and the injunction that women should keep silent in church. Thus the problem of voice for European women was acute since their culture defined them as incompetent in or irrelevant to two core areas of speculation about life, politics and theology. Nonetheless the monastic tradition provided women with enclaves of self-direction, albeit at the price of entry into a closed religious community.

It was within the special enclave of religious life that the tradition of Western European women's autobiography was first established, in narratives about the autobiographer's relationship with God. Such a tradition, involving a relationship with a first cause, did not permit the development of the sense of agency and acting on one's own behalf with which the Greek ideal of the hero is infused. Instead, it promoted meditation about the nature of God and the recording of direct experience of divine illumination.

This tradition is manifested in the writing of medieval women religious like the twelfth-century German abbess Hildegard of Bingen. A composer of liturgical music and songs, a playwright, a healer and a builder of institutions, Hildegard records an inner life devoted to surrender of the will and to ecstatic visions such as the sycamore tree she observes dancing outside her window on a gray winter day. The totally nonverbal visionary experience gives her the sense that she and everything she knew or could imagine are present in the sycamore's preternaturally beautiful movements.[5]

Dame Julian of Norwich, a fourteenth-century British religious, gives her reader the same sense of rejoicing in intense and deeply reassuring nonverbal contact with God. In her *Book of Shewings to the Anchoress Julian of Norwich* (1393), she doesn't engage in mental calisthenics about how it is possible to know God. Instead she provides a record of the visions she has received during her life of prayer and meditation, and some practical encouragement to others to follow in her footsteps. She is highly literate and possesses a formidable knowledge of Scripture, but it is the vision of God she wants to convey rather than how she felt about it. She can speculate about God's being a point fitting within the palm of her hand and yet present everywhere, or some other equally abstract object within whom all human affairs are subsumed. She conveys wonder, delight and confidence in God's Providence ("And all Shall be well, and all manner of thing shall be well") but shows no concern for her own agency.[6]

St. Teresa of Avila, a High Renaissance Spanish mystic, extends this tradition in her beguiling *Life of St. Teresa by Herself* (1562–65). In it she uses the image of a garden being fed by streams of water to convey her sense of the operation of grace in her consciousness. Her guide to her readers on the techniques of prayer and meditation is practical and vividly written. Her entire history is a story of a relationship with God, although her powers of expression make every monk, nun, confessor and family member live in the reader's mind. She is direct and plainspoken about the insignificance of the will in coming to know God:

*All that the soul has to do at these times of quiet is merely to be
calm and make no noise. By noise I mean working with the intellect to find great numbers of words and reflections with which
to thank God for this blessing. . . . The will must quietly and
wisely understand that we cannot deal violently with God; and
that our efforts are like great logs of wood indiscriminately piled
on [a fire], which will only put out the spark. . . . Let it speak
any words of love that suggest themselves, in the firm and sure
knowledge that what it says is the truth. But let it pay no attention to the intellect, which is merely being tiresome.*[7]

The mystic's direct experience of the springs of life which flow
through a divinely created world came to men also, as the writing
of St. Teresa's friend and protégé St. John of the Cross demon-
strates. But women's accounts of their mystical experience set
the pattern for describing a woman's life in a way that shaped
women's subsequent narratives as definitively as the odyssey gave
the underlying form to male autobiography.

The secularization of European culture produced no female
Rousseau, claiming to be the model of a new social and political
type for a life to be understood in terms of this world. Even had she
existed, we may argue that the silencing of women on matters of
politics and theology would have required a structure for her story
different from Rousseau's self-absorbed narrative of his own creation. The secular form of women's narratives emerged in the
bourgeois preoccupation with romantic love, marriage, family and
property.

We see the transitional version of this life plot in the narratives
of women like the Duchess of Newcastle, intent on presenting the
history of her family and her own aspirations as aspects of family
history. Though her concerns are political and intellectual, and always highly individualistic, she relates them through family and
marriage. Hers is an aristocratic voice: secular, ambitious, strong-
willed, finding a place defined by family and status on which to
stand to comment on her experience.

The archetypal form for the bourgeois female history came in
the early nineteenth century from the secularized romance, the
life plot linking the erotic quest for the ideal mate with property
and social mobility. Within the ideal type of the romantic plot

given early expression in Rousseau's *Émile* (1762), the female heroine is a creature of pure emotion and little intellect, who exists to become the perfect mate for the self-creating hero. Her life history ends when she encounters him, because her existence thereafter is subsumed within his.

The consuming bourgeois preoccupation with erotic adventure, family, property and the primacy of the emotional fulfillment of private life led to the transformation of the female life plot from the visionary encounter with God, a God often viewed in extremely abstract terms, to the quest for the ideal hero, a quest which gave shape to the fiction, theater, opera and ballet of nineteenth-century Europe. In that story what is important about the female is not her agency but the quality of her emotional response, a quality celebrated in opera and dance, or in fiction as passionate as Alessandro Manzoni's *I promessi sposi* (1825–1827) or as cool as Jane Austen's *Pride and Prejudice* (1813).

The conventions of the romance require that the heroine be courted, and the dynamic of the plot comes from the way in which the barriers to expressing her response to the hero—scheming relatives, class constraints, opposing political forces, the social prescriptions of race and caste—are progressively removed by fate, destiny or other external forces over which the heroine has no control, so that the final ecstatic union with the beloved may occur. This shaping romantic myth is, of course, a Western creation; it is a source of puzzlement to members of non-Western societies, in which marriage operates to link family, property and political or religious groups, or else as a prudential institution guaranteeing personal service and the care of one generation for another.

What is important about the Western romantic heroine is that she has no agency, or power to act on her own behalf. Things happen to her—adventures, lovers, reversals of fortune. She has an antitype, the scheming woman, who does try to create her own destiny, like Becky Sharp in Thackeray's *Vanity Fair* (1847–48), or the kind of woman concerned with politics who made her way to the guillotine during the French Revolution, whether monarch like Marie Antoinette or liberal reformer like Madame Roland. But such figures were held up as negative models of unseemly ambition.

The wave of humanitarian concern for human beings exploited

by slavery, the cruelties of child labor or insensitivity to the feelings and needs of the insane did give indirect encouragement to a new kind of woman autobiographer, the escaped female slave who could ignore the social taboos governing speaking about female sexuality by recounting histories of sexual exploitation by white slaveowners. Abolitionists encouraged memoirs of the slavewoman's journey to freedom, often epic in its privations and dangers. These stories by strong women presented no threat to gender categories because they fit with the image of the slave as victim, and because white readers could feel secure that such strength was safely contained within the boundaries of racial subordination. The frontierswoman's narrative, a counterpart to the male imperial experience, could not be so fully embodied as the slavewoman's, for the proprieties required that women never speak of the dangers of giving birth far from the services of midwives or the suffering of the breast abscess which had to be lanced by the patient herself. So, although the frontierswoman's strength was called upon daily, she never recorded it, and in keeping silence allowed her life to seem like a domestic romance.

By the second half of the nineteenth century, women's access to education and the emergence of the women's professions provided a new social territory from which women could examine the meaning of their lives and comment upon their society. Many stories of women's struggle for education and successful battles with discrimination might well have fitted the Horatio Alger model of a life devoted to the unremitting quest for success, for many educated women gained national stature and exercised considerable power through the institutions they founded, colleges like Bryn Mawr, hospitals like the renowned Philadelphia Hospital for Women and reform associations like the National Consumers' League. But they did not create or control great fortunes, so their power was discreetly veiled in good works. Like the frontierswomen silent about their physical strength and courage, pioneer women professionals were silent about their ambitions and recounted their lives as though their successes just happened to them, rather like the soprano's chance meeting with the tenor in the first act of an opera. So the woman professional, actually a new and potentially revolutionary social type, told her story as a philanthropic romance: she seems to have chanced upon the causes which elicit a lifetime commitment from her. She never acknowledges strategizing about how to advance the cause; she is as surprised as anyone else when success is at hand. The life plot contrived by these silences is not one of rags to riches but rather a modified romance in which service motivations replace erotic passions as the governing force in life.

What are we to make of such silences? Should we agree that the Western cultural mirror distorts women's self-perception so that they cannot see their own agency? Can women really not adapt Plato and Aristotle to suit themselves so that they can reflect on their own political life? Are they not capable of forging their own tradition for the expression of political motives? Clearly this is not the case, because frontierswomen and pioneer women reformers kept diaries and wrote letters which dealt with their physical bodies, openly acknowledged the wish for power and depicted the writers as political beings. So the problem is one of censorship for public self-presentation. Every autobiographer wants to persuade others to learn from her or his life. Most aim to convince their readers to take up some important cause, follow a new spiritual path, be aware of particular hazards, develop a new moral sense. To achieve this they cannot depart too dramatically from popularly accepted stereotypes which affirm the man of action and the suffering or redemptive female. To do so is to risk losing their persuasive power. So the private mirror works as well for women as for men, but the public one may be another matter. Of course men may also censor their softer selves when describing their life journeys, editing out the tears or despair, eliding the help of others, making the hesitant course seem the path of firm resolve. Rembrandt's sixty-two self-portraits suggest that the cultural mirror could give trouble to men also, even so gifted and original an artist as Rembrandt.

Of course, in theory the modern practice of psychiatry encourages the most rigorous scrutiny of conventional life plots, so that the public and private selves can negotiate some sort of entente cordiale. But the founders of psychiatry, Freud and Jung, inscribed the conventional male and female life scripts so thoroughly into the practice of their art that a profession based on scrutiny of life histories has not yet come up with more accurate or revealing cultural mirrors.

What makes the reading of autobiography so appealing is the chance it offers to see how this man or that woman whose public self interests us has negotiated the problem of self-awareness and has broken the internalized code a culture supplies about how life should be experienced. Most of us, unless faced with emotional illness, don't give our inner life scripts a fraction of the attention we give to the plots of movies or TV specials about some person of prominence. Yet the need to examine our inherited scripts is just beneath the surface of consciousness, so that while we think we are reading a gripping story, what really grips us is the inner reflection on our own lives the autobiographer sets in motion.

But why should just one literary genre preempt this area of self-reflection today? Our grandparents and great-grandparents were moved to it by reading the Bible, and by reading the works of Dostoevsky, Dickens and George Eliot. They could reflect on causation in human affairs by reading about Darwinian biology, geology, the observations of field botanists. They could, if they chose, read philosophers like John Stuart Mill, Bertrand Russell or John Dewey, who wrote a kind of standard English which any educated person could understand. If they were of a psychological bent, they could read William James; if literary, Matthew Arnold. The entire span of humanistic inquiry about what it means to be human, how the individual is shaped by society, whether she or he ever has free will, what shapes the imagination, what talents are valued and what misunderstood, how great political figures are formed and how they resonate with their followers—all such questions were, until recently, analyzed in a humanistic discourse which was accessible to an interested reader.

Today, autobiography is almost the only kind of writing which tackles such questions in language a nonspecialist can read with ease. The technical language of history, psychology, literary criticism, philosophy is a necessary accompaniment of the effort to reach an ever more exact formulation of complex problems. But it also shuts out the nonspecialist, and makes it nearly impossible for such a person to draw on those modern disciplines for the scrutiny of her or his own life. If we think of St. Augustine's *Confessions* and try to imagine him using the language of cathexis and significant others to convey the experience of conversion, we know he would not reach the audience he has for some 1,600 years. If we imagine readers of *The Old Curiosity Shop* grappling with the concept of alterity, we know they would not have been there poised at the dock, waiting for the next installment of Little Nell's life. If we think of Rousseau offering statistical calculations of the likelihood that his experience correlated closely with that of other men of his generation in France, we see his claims to be a "new man" differently. But his autobiography tells us, sometimes in too much detail, just how it felt to him. And that magical opportunity of entering another life is what really sets us thinking about our own.

CHAPTER TWO

THE SECULAR HERO

WHEN JEAN-JACQUES ROUSSEAU (1712–1778) completed his *Confessions* in 1770 he introduced the secular hero into European literature and recounted his own life in a form and style which influenced male life histories well into the twentieth century. Rousseau set the pattern which required the autobiographer to record the shaping influences of his childhood and the emotions of his maturity. But even as Rousseau set down his denunciation of aristocratic privilege and contrasted his real emotional life with received values, an American contemporary, Benjamin Franklin (1706–1790), was forging another male life plot, which preempted much of the foreground of nineteenth-century male autobiography. Franklin's self-presentation defined for the first time the archetypal figure of the capitalist hero, rebellious against inherited privilege, scornful of inefficiency and of waste, driven by economic motives which never figured in Rousseau's wildest dreams. While Rousseau wanted to compel an inattentive society to recognize his literary and dramatic genius, Franklin describes himself as content to accumulate wealth, and to instruct the rest of the world about the moral and economic qualities which earned him his wealth, and through it status and public recognition.

Franklin tells us he wasted no time railing against the loss of family or the failures of judgment which slowed down his meteoric rise to success. While Rousseau seems never to have been able to forget what might have been had the fates been kinder or he wiser, Franklin claims to have set about controlling himself and his destiny from very early youth. He began by teaching himself the skills his unquenchable curiosity alerted him were needed to manage his life in the swiftly changing environment of eighteenth-century America, and he seems to have expected that no one else could take on that responsibility for him.

Rousseau blames a doting family for his uncontrollable emotions.

> *Thus there began to form in me . . . a heart at once proud and affectionate, and a character effeminate and inflexible, which by always wavering between weakness and courage, between self-indulgence and virtue, has throughout my life set me in conflict with myself, to such effect that abstinence and enjoyment, pleasure and prudence have alike eluded me.*[1]

Franklin has no such complaint. Self-taught in rhetoric and logic, he tells us he quickly found the models on which to build his capacity for public debate.

> *While I was intent on improving my language, I met with an English Grammar (I think it was Greenwood's) at the end of which there were two little Sketches of the Arts of Rhetoric and Logic, the latter finishing with a Specimen of a Dispute in the Socratic method. And soon after I procur'd Xenophon's Memorable Things of Socrates, wherein there are many instances of the same Method. . . . I took a Delight in it, practis'd it continually and grew very artful and expert.*[2]

There is no hint here of the longing for a skilled teacher who might have helped perfect Franklin's style of argument. He wants the reader to believe that all he learned was through his own agency, mastered quickly and deployed without misconstruction or error.

If we are to believe Franklin, the war between emotion and intellect never broke out for him. He was a man who could report his plan to arrive at moral perfection with a straight face, and with no hint of self-mockery.

It was at this time that I conceiv'd the bold and arduous Project of arriving at moral Perfection. I wish'd to live without commiting any Fault at any time; I would conquer all that either Natural Inclination, Custom, or Company might lead me into. As I knew, or thought I knew, what was right and wrong, I did not see why I might not always do the one and avoid the other.[3]

While he admits that his scheme for eradicating all moral failure in his life did not succeed completely, he reports, with pragmatic self-satisfaction, that the effort made him a better and happier man. Temperance gave him health. Industry and frugality led to early wealth. Sincerity and love of justice earned him public trust and acclaim.

Old insults and indignities seem never to have sapped Franklin's energies, as they continually did those of Rousseau, because, by acquiring wealth, Franklin knew he could compel respect from those who had mistreated him. So, after fleeing Boston to escape the beatings of his older brother, to whom Franklin was apprenticed, he erased the indignity on his first visit home by flaunting his affluence in front of his brother's apprentices.

I went to see him at his Printing-House: I was better dress'd than ever while in his Service. Having a genteel new Suit from Head to foot, a Watch, and my Pockets lin'd with near Five Pounds Sterling in Silver. He receiv'd me not very frankly, look'd me all over, and turned to his Work again.[4]

To rub in his success Franklin showed his silver coins and watch to his former fellow apprentices and underlined his changed circumstances by giving them money to drink his health.

Naturally, such conduct didn't cement brotherly ties, something which Franklin gives the appearance of having cared little about. Perhaps because he abandoned family and took charge of navigating his own life course at a very early age, Franklin placed a correspondingly high value on voluntary association, from the Junto—an association of fellow clerks and apprentices which he formed in Philadelphia for mutual self-instruction—to the libraries, philosophical societies, orphanages, hospitals and the University of Pennsylvania which were the institutions that claimed his energies as a mature man. These figure largely in his memoir, though his wife and the son who died at the age of four each rate only one mention.

When he speaks of happiness, it is public recognition rather than domestic pleasure which excites Franklin's comment. When his wealth was established on a secure foundation, Franklin tells us he withdrew from business, expecting to use his leisure in scientific and philosophical inquiry. Instead, he became a public figure. Elected an alderman and a member of the legislature and appointed a justice of the peace, Franklin tells us he rejoiced in an enlarged power for doing good but also in the sweetness of the public acclaim.

> *I would not however insinuate that my Ambition was not flatter'd by all these Promotions. It certainly was. For considering my low Beginning they were great Things to me.*[5]

Equally gratifying was the recognition he received as a scientist. Snubbed by the British Royal Society for his reports of experiments with electricity, Franklin lived to be elected an honorary member once his method for extracting electricity from clouds had been demonstrated to the French court at Marly. He tells the reader that his successful experiments gave him "infinite pleasure," as did the spread of his reputation among Europe's best scientific minds.

The life story Franklin lays out downplays the rebellious, argumentative and brash boy; accentuates childhood poverty and lack of schooling and exaggerates the laziness and thriftlessness of those he bested in business. The force which gives momentum to Franklin's narrative is the story of his self-education and progress in self-discipline. In such a narrative there is no place for the emotions of family, for sexual passion or the other human appetites. Indeed Franklin was able to humiliate an employer by pledging them both to a vegetarian diet, something which caused him no distress but was extremely difficult for his companion.

Not surprisingly, Franklin's mature pleasures were intellectual or they came from calculating how far he had come from what he calls "my low Beginning." He seems a cold fish beside the romantic, emotionally solipsistic Rousseau, who proclaims,

The first, the greatest, the strongest, the most inextinguishable of all my needs was entirely one of the heart. It was the need for intimate companionship, for a companionship as intimate as possible, which was the chief reason why I needed a woman rather than a man. . . . This singular need was such that the most intimate physical union could not fulfill it; only two souls in the same body would have sufficed. Failing that I always felt a void.[6]

The void which lies at the center of the romantic quest for union with the beloved, and the contrasting but less passionate pleasures of the entrepreneur, and later the professional, emerged in the late eighteenth and nineteenth centuries as central themes in white male life histories. These two modes of individualistic fulfillment flourished around the twin poles of domesticity and capitalism, the two shaping institutions of modern bourgeois culture. When Freud described love and work as mankind's two governing emotions, his observations were drawn from the study of bourgeois institutions, though he believed himself to be articulating universal truths. Medieval Europe or samurai Japan might have required including the emotions of the warrior and the monk, and a later perspective would have required including the joys of the bureaucrat and the scientist's drive to conquer nature. The modern tradition of autobiography has flourished around the conflicts between love and work, with work assuming center stage in American writing until the cultural rebellions of the midtwentieth century.

These two themes merge in the life histories of the black men for whom slavery or racial exploitation made either quest an epic struggle against overwhelming odds. So the other great male narrative of modernity, the escape of the black man from slavery, merges these themes in a single passionate narrative of self-creation within a society in which property and status were the defining elements of the self. Frederick Douglass (1817–1895), the most articulate chronicler of the male American runaway slave's experience, begins the account of his life by showing the reader an inner world of emotional and physical suffering, and grief at betrayal, which is charged with romantic passion. As a man whose every word must further the cause of the Abolition movement, he strives successfully to make the reader feel the blows of harsh and cruel masters, the horror of the childhood discovery that someone owned him and would shortly tear him from the love and security of his grandmother's cabin.

But, unlike the runaway apprentice Franklin, Douglass faced torture and death for his efforts at freedom, and the underlying psychological drama of his life history is the process by which he overcame that fear and learned to fight back against his oppressors. In the language of modern criticism we see his story shift from being acted upon to exercising agency. Like Franklin, Douglass taught himself to read and modeled his style on the examples of great rhetoric he encountered in a school text purchased without his owner's knowledge. But Douglass's learning was an illicit activity, for which he faced serious penalties, and it was one which allowed him to learn that slavery was not a divinely ordered institution but the product of human greed.

> "Slaveholders," thought I, "are only a band of successful robbers, who, leaving their own homes, went into Africa for the purpose of stealing and reducing my people to slavery." . . . I loathed them as the meanest and most wicked of men. . . . I wished myself a beast, a bird, anything rather than a slave. I was wretched and gloomy beyond my ability to describe. This everlasting thinking distressed and tormented me; and yet there was no getting rid of this subject of my thoughts.[7]

Douglass's rejection of the slave mentality and inner disgust with the treatment meted out by his supposedly Christian owners led to his being sent to work on the plantation of a brutal master famous for his ability to "break" the most fractious black field hands. It was here that the seventeen-year-old Douglass endured his most terrible beatings and eventually summoned the courage to resist.

> Whence came the daring spirit necessary to grapple with a man who, eight-and-forty hours before, could, with his slightest word, have made me tremble like a leaf in a storm, I do not know; at any rate I was resolved to fight, and what was better still I actually was hard at it. The fighting madness had come upon me, and I found my strong fingers firmly attached to the

*throat of the tyrant, as heedless of consequences, at the moment,
as if we stood as equals before the law. The very color of the man
was forgotten. I felt as supple as a cat and was ready for him at
every turn. . . . The battle with Mr. Covey, undignified as it was
and as I fear my narration of it is, was the turning point of my
"life as a slave." It rekindled in my breast the smoldering embers
of liberty.*[8]

After this epic resistance, the reader knows that in time Douglass will find his way to freedom. After the suspense of an abortive attempt, the moment arrived in Douglass's twenty-first year when he departed dressed as a sailor, carrying the identification papers of a friendly free seaman. Once on free soil Douglass felt he lived as intensely in one day as he had in all his previous twenty-one years. He made connections with the Underground Railroad, sent for the free black woman he planned to marry and set out for New Bedford, where he expected to use his trade of caulker in the thriving shipping industry.

At this point in his narrative, when he is free to make his way in the world, Douglass's tone changes. His inner life recedes from focus, and it is an economic and political man who speaks in a voice not unlike Franklin's. Like Franklin, Douglass was formidable in industry, and like him he was tireless in self-education. Excluded from practicing his craft by the racial prejudice of white ship workers, Douglass eventually obtained regular work in a foundry. Working a heavy bellows, standing above the molten metal of a brass foundry, Douglass said he "often nailed a newspaper to the post near my bellows and read" while he worked.

Three years later Douglass's career as a speaker and writer for the Abolitionist cause began. Very quickly his eloquence, intelligence and polemical skills made his audiences question whether he had ever been a slave—prompting Douglass to write the history of his experience of slavery and to describe his escape. The public avowal increased his impact as a speaker but also multiplied the risk that he would be recaptured and returned to slavery.

Running the risk made him a public figure, a spokesman for his race and a key figure in the emerging issues of race relations posed by secession and the Civil War. When, as the fortunes of war turned against the Union, the decision was reached to raise two black regiments in Massachusetts, it was Douglass who was asked to aid in the recruitment and Douglass who decided to call upon President Lincoln to redress the situation when the black regiments encountered white hostility, met brutal retaliation from Confederate soldiers and were paid far less than other Union troops. Entering the White House for the meeting, Douglass, like Franklin, stopped to remember his beginnings:

> *I was an ex-slave, identified with a despised race, and yet I was to meet the most exalted person in the great republic.*[9]

As the symbolic hero who represented the struggles of his people during the battle to abolish slavery, Douglass suffered a crisis of identity after the conclusion of the Civil War and the extension of the vote to African-American males. Very quickly he discovered that emancipation and the franchise did not mean former slaves had gained equality, and that his powers of rhetoric were still needed for the cause. Not surprisingly, his most popular lecture on the lyceum, college and university circuit was on the subject of the "self-made man." He could tell that story in a different key from the usual Horatio Alger narrative of youthful poverty, self-education and economic success. His was an emotional journey, in which, at least by the closing years of his life, success had begun to seem very ambiguous.

When his speaking tours took him back to Maryland, he found himself speaking in the courthouse beside the Easton jail where he had been imprisoned for his abortive first break for freedom. When attending a parade in Baltimore, he met the daughter of the woman who had opposed the rules of her slaveowning family and helped him learn to read. He was even asked to visit his former owner, whom he had hated as being utterly without human feeling, when the old man was approaching death and wanted to make peace with him.

Along with these unsettling encounters came the disillusionments of discovering that though the Civil War was over the battle to overcome racial prejudice had barely begun. This recognition makes the ending of Douglass's account of his life diminuendo, without the tone of self-satisfaction which permeates Franklin's memoir. An agent of his people? A self-made man? A hero who has confronted and overcome slavery? Yes, but for what? is the unanswered question behind the surface account of success Douglass offers in the Franklin mode.

Nineteenth-century American male memoirs replicate these patterns with remarkable regularity. Andrew Carnegie (1835–1919) writes like a latter-day Franklin about the same unrelenting effort to accumulate wealth, and about the fulfillments of reaching a stage in life when he can retire from business and devote himself to study and philanthropy.[10] Like Franklin he lacks any sense of self-mockery, so that he can blandly present himself as an expert on labor relations when in fact, because of the management's ruthless strikebreaking, his steel companies were the breeding grounds for America's most militant unions.

Franklin, the eighteenth-century self-educated savant, was replaced in the nineteenth century by a new kind of self-educated man, the engineer and inventor, a man whose account of his life is charged with agency and whose purpose, like Franklin's, is to teach those who follow after him the principles of self-creation. In *My Life and Work* (1922) Henry Ford (1863–1947), the eccentric, chatty and opinionated creator of the modern mass automobile market, states his purpose as an autobiographer with admirable precision.

> *I am not outlining the career of the Ford Motor Company for any personal reason. . . . What I am trying to emphasize is that the ordinary way of doing business is not the best way.[11]*

The best way, as laid out by Ford, was the mass production of a standard product, delivered to the market at a price that the person of average income could afford. Ford was the archetypal engineer, who could see the application of his ideas about automobile production to the full range of products consumed in a democratic society.

> *I am now most interested in fully demonstrating that the ideas we have put into practice are capable of the largest application—that they have nothing peculiarly to do with motor cars or tractors but form something in the nature of a universal code.[12]*

The challenges to be overcome on Ford's odyssey are not the challenges of the Greek hero; they are mistaken views of economics, corporate finance, business and engineering design. They begin with Ford's farmer father, who paid him (to little effect) to stop tinkering with machines, and continue in the persons of shortsighted managers like those of the Detroit Electric Company, who offered him promotion to the "general superintendency" of the company, on condition that he give up working on his internal combustion engine. The *I* who speaks in Ford's narrative is totally charged with agency, a sure captain of his destiny, who never hesitates.

> *I had to choose between my job and my automobile. I chose the automobile, or rather I gave up the job—for there was really nothing in the way of a choice.*[13]

Ford's wife features in the narrative in two places. He takes his father's gift of land, supposedly an incentive to stop tinkering with machines, to provide the income that enables him to marry. And when he abandons his well-paid job to work exclusively on automobile design, Mrs. Ford agrees wholeheartedly. Otherwise the characters in the narrative are machines, or people who got in the way of Ford's ambition to build "a car that would meet the wants of the multitudes."

Very few signs of emotion creep into the narrative, except Ford's perpetual exasperation with people who want to found companies to make money rather than to make first-class products. When he does show feeling, it concerns machines. In 1903 he and a colleague, Tom Cooper, designed and built two racing cars, both generating eighty horsepower, an unheard of capacity at the time. "The roar of those cylinders alone was enough to half kill a man," he writes.

> *There was only one seat. One life to a car was enough. I tried out the cars. Cooper tried out the cars. We let them out at full speed. I cannot quite describe the sensation. Going over Niagara Falls would have been but a pastime after a ride in one of them.*[14]

By the concluding chapters of *My Life and Work* Ford openly acknowledges that business is a religion for him.

> *There is something sacred about a big business which provides a living for hundreds and thousands of families. When one looks about at the babies coming into the world, at the boys and girls going to school, at the young workingmen, who, on the strength of their jobs, are marrying and setting up for themselves, at the thousands of homes that are being paid for on installments out of the earnings of men—when one looks at a great productive organization that is enabling all these things to be done, then the continuance of the business becomes a holy trust. It becomes greater and more important than the individuals.* [15]

In his concluding chapters he objects most strenuously to those who think luck or economic circumstances have helped the Ford Motor Company build its worldwide business. There was no agency involved but his own. Not luck but the correctness of his engineering ideas built the enterprise that now seems sacred to him. In Ford's construction of his life, we can see the completely secular hero, certain that through progress in science and engineering "we shall learn to be masters rather than servants of Nature." He sees himself as one of the future masters, and his life as a model for planning the emerging society of mass production. The claim to agency over nature as well as in human affairs takes the life plot of the secular hero about as far from St. Augustine and Rousseau as it is possible to travel. The hero's journey is now a technical odyssey, not a spiritual or emotional quest. Indeed Ford's most powerful emotions were linked to machines, not to the vision of God or an earthly paradise of the emotions.

The life history of W. E. B. Du Bois (1868–1963) starts out as a Franklin-style account of self-creation. We see the author orphaned in early youth in what he describes as a sunny corner of New England, guiltily relieved after his mother's death because he was now free to give single-minded attention to his ambitions. At seventeen, just as he began to register that racial feelings might undermine his childhood friendship with white schoolmates in his home town of Great Barrington, several churches in the region

supported him to study at Fisk University in Tennessee, and a
wealthy white woman agreed to pay for his books. Carried far away
from his New England roots by this community generosity, Du
Bois became an African-American during his years at Fisk, years
marked less by intellectual awakening than by the discovery of his
people. Thereafter Du Bois describes his life as a quest, first for
knowledge to teach the rest of American society about the results
of racial discrimination and then for an institutional base from
which he can wage war on white racism and help defend his people from lynch law's violent rule.

The first stage of the quest required rigorous preparation of the
mind, first at Harvard and then at the University of Berlin. At these
preeminent institutions, Du Bois expected literally to gain the
tools of social and political analysis which would aid him in freeing
his people from racial oppression. A freethinker, he describes himself as the model Enlightenment scholar, a believer in progress
through education and the use of human reason. In Cambridge
and Berlin his youthful emotions were rigidly disciplined to focus
on the task, although in Europe, on some magical occasions, he
found himself free to be friends with whites, particularly white
women, outside the rigid racial system of the United States.

On his return to the United States from Berlin, Du Bois was
the pure type of the professional scholar, ready to use his mind to
liberate his race. But prejudice against black scholars sent this
eager social scientist to an unlikely and half-comical setting for an
apostle of rational progress. Wilberforce University, where Du Bois
describes his first academic job, was one of the key institutions of
the African Methodist Episcopal Church, committed to evangelical emotion and spiritual uplift. There Du Bois quickly became a
defender of academic values against the nepotism of the ruling
AME bishop, who found him suspect both for his views on religion
and for his refusal to toe the line of the ruling political hierarchy.
For a twenty-five-year-old eagerly contemplating marriage, the
recognition that his days at Wilberforce were numbered might
have been daunting, but the quest allowed Du Bois no self-pity.

My first quarter century of life seems to me . . . as singularly
well aimed at a certain goal, along a clearly planned path. I re-

turned, ready and eager to begin a life-work, leading to the emancipation of the American Negro. History and the other social sciences were to be my weapons, to be sharpened and applied by research and writing. Where and how was the question in 1895. I became uneasy about my life-program. I had published my first book, but I was doing nothing directly in the social sciences and saw no immediate prospect. Then the door of opportunity opened: just a crack, to be sure, but a distinct opening.[16]

Du Bois was too well trained a historian to claim total agency for himself, but he presents himself as always ready for the slightest opportunity to pursue the cause. "I did not hesitate for an instant," he reports, telling of the ambiguous appointment at the University of Pennsylvania which opened up, "but reported for duty with a complete plan of work and outline of methods and aims and even proposed schedules to be filled out." At Penn he began his life of serious scholarship, always pursued as though the research were its own justification, and the slights of white faculty insignificant.

I began a more clearly planned career, which had an unusual measure of success, but was in the end pushed aside by forces which, if not entirely beyond my control, were yet of great weight.[17]

The forces were indeed beyond his control. His life history takes on tragic overtones as its brilliant narrator, inspired by the rise of the research ideal which American scholars imported from Germany in the 1890s, is forced to concede that there are no sponsors for his research goals within the American academy or among its philanthropic supporters, and certainly none within black academic institutions.

At first, on moving to Atlanta University, where Du Bois worked from his twenty-ninth to his forty-second birthday, he still felt in control of what he called his "life-program." He was working consciously against the evangelical culture of uplift which characterized black universities, to create a program of "scientific investigation into social conditions, primarily for scientific ends."[18] He had a grand vision of transforming people's understanding of the Negro from a set of poorly understood "problems" to questions which could be refined and sharpened through access to an unimpeachable database, which he would create.

That vision faded before the reality of Atlanta's race riots and the shocking discovery that there was no demand for the kind of rigorously researched data that Du Bois wanted to establish. What white Americans wanted to sponsor was the ideal of a docile black population trained in the manual arts, whose psychic energy would continue to be channeled through the religious mode of spiritual uplift. And there were black leaders like Booker T. Washington who thought just such an educational framework was the more effective strategy for the times. Their success forced Du Bois to consider the social basis of thought and to begin the intellectual journey toward Marxism which shaped the second half of his life.

In his narrative Du Bois inserts a chapter describing his character at age fifty, an assessment followed by comments from the perspective of the writer in the 1960s, when he was well into his ninth decade. He thought himself honest, thrifty, emotionally unfulfilled except through his work.

> My wife and children were incidents of my main life work. I was not neglectful of my family; I furnished a good home. . . . But my main work was out in the world and not at home.[19]

A shy man, conscious of every slight against his blackness, he deliberately turned away from knowing many of his great contemporaries, and the same shyness made him know his students only as intellects and not as human beings. Thus the man of reason assesses the price paid for becoming the philosopher for his race and his society. It is an assessment Benjamin Franklin could not have made, and it overlooks the emotional range of Du Bois's response to his generation of black artists and writers, whose work he published and fostered when he moved to New York in 1910 to edit *The Crisis*, the publication of the newly founded NAACP.

The second half of Du Bois's life was clouded by the fear of radical ideas which shaped the perceptions of both whites and blacks about his further projects for research and his efforts at building a Pan-African response to the issues of race and imperialism which were central to international relations from the 1930s to the 1960s. The Depression brought him to the study of Marxism, and the 1939–45 War was a moment of historical illumination.

> *When the depression came and thousands of workers, black and white, were starving in the 30's, I began to awake and to see in the socialism of the New Deal, emancipation for all workers, and the labor problem which included the negro problem. I knew that Hitler and Mussolini were fighting communism, and using race prejudice to make some white people rich and all colored peoples poor. But it was not until later that I realized that the colonialism of Great Britain and France had exactly the same object and methods as the fascists and the Nazis were trying clearly to use.*[20]

Certain of his own intellectual integrity, Du Bois was repeatedly astonished that his proposed courses on Marxism at Atlanta University, or his opposition to nuclear war, and his role in founding the Peace Information Center in New York, were perceived as efforts to spread propaganda for the Soviet Union. His indictment and trial on criminal charges for having failed to register as an agent of a foreign power (McCarthy-speak for the Soviet Union) left him crushed and virtually silenced, even though immediately acquitted. In his isolation he finally drops the persona of detached social scientist and describes himself as a redemptive savior of his people.

> *I bowed before the storm. But I did not break. I continued to speak and write when and where I could. I faced my lowered income and lived within it. I found new friends and lived in a wider world than ever before—a world with no color line. I lost my leadership of my race. It was a dilemma for the mass of Negroes; either they joined the current beliefs and actions of most whites or they could not make a living or hope for preferment. Preferment was possible. The color line was beginning to break. Negroes were getting recognition as never before. Was not the*

sacrifice of one man small payment for this? Even those who
disagreed with this judgement at least kept quiet. The colored
children ceased to hear my name.[21]

The last sentence of searing grief marks Du Bois's transformation in his own mind from secular hero to semireligious redemptive figure. He might have surrendered personal agency, but he
clung to the idea that his life was in tune with the larger forces of
history. It was a view of life closer to that of later heroes of colonial
liberation outside the United States than to the individualistic
rationalism with which his story began.

The struggle to maintain a sense of personal agency when confronted with economic and political forces which overwhelm personal ambition is the leitmotiv of twentieth-century narratives by
capitalist heroes of accumulation. Lee Iacocca's story of his life in
the automobile industry presents a striking contrast to the narrative of the founder of the industry. Henry Ford's life revolved
around machines. He was scornful of the emerging world of corporate finance, interested in the nuts and bolts of building things.
His memoir is interspersed with essays on the process of cast-
ing metal, on the five thousand parts, "screws, nuts and all," in
a Ford car and the best ways of soldering a radiator. Lee Iacocca
(b. 1924), one of the most successful presidents of the Ford Motor
Company in the 1970s, studied engineering but quickly transferred from his engineering traineeship at Ford into marketing.

I was nine months into the program with another nine to go.
But engineering no longer interested me. The day I'd arrived,
they had me designing a clutch spring. It had taken me an en-
tire day to make a detailed drawing of it, and I said to myself
"What on earth am I doing? Is this how I want to be spending
the rest of my life?" I wanted to stay at Ford, but not in engineer-
ing. I was eager to be where the real action was—marketing and
sales. I liked working with people more than machines.[22]

Iacocca represents the new-style leader created by the economy of
consumption, in which engineering and production can be taken
for granted, and the path to achievement lies in understanding and
stimulating consumption.

Iacocca's story reads like the traditional immigrant tale of success in the promised land of opportunity. He could be a Horatio Alger character for the first half of the memoir—energetic, strong willed, determined to succeed. Working with people meant learning how to communicate with them and provide the proper motivation. He went to the Dale Carnegie Institute and learned how to be an effective public speaker, and how to win the loyalty of employees.

> *In corporate life, you have to encourage all your people to make a contribution to the common good and come up with better ways of doing things. You don't have to accept every single suggestion, but if you don't get back to the guy and say "Hey, that idea was terrific," and pat him on the back, he'll never give you another one. That kind of communication lets people know they really count.*[23]

Soon he was a youthful general manager of the Ford Division, eagerly studying demography and poring over market research about the tastes of the rising baby boom generation. His ideas about the Mustang concerned style, comfort and price—its new look would sit on an existing platform and engine. Its resounding success brought Iacocca into the inner sanctum of the Ford Motor Company, as vice president of the corporate car and truck group.

His skill as a promoter of Ford products and his understanding of the styling which would appeal to customers made him a strong candidate for the presidency of the company, but now, as a member of the inner corporate circle, he had to come to terms with the company's controlling stockholder and chairman. Henry Ford II represented the kind of power Iacocca had not yet had to deal with, and he realized much too late that the ensuing clash of wills could have only one outcome.

But at first the experience of power was heady. He has only to list what his responsibilities encompassed: 432,000 employees, a payroll of $3.5 billion, sales of $14.9 billion, profits of $515 million. His energy was prodigious. Costs were cut to boost earnings, losing businesses disposed of, control systems tightened up. He thought he was part of a modern version of a royal court ("If Henry was king, I was the crown prince"), but he failed to grasp that

Henry Ford controlled the succession, and that he might not relish so high performing an heir apparent.

After the blow fell and he was dismissed in 1978, Iacocca realized that he had ignored the Ford Motor Company's history. He should have analyzed the situation better—he had known that all his predecessors had been summarily dismissed for captious reasons, but he'd fooled himself into believing that he would be different. Worse still, after his dismissal the Ford executives he'd believed were friends never spoke to him again. "It really makes you ask yourself the big questions," this basically unreflective man writes.

> If I could do it over, could I have protected my family better? The pressure on them was awful. You watch your wife get sicker—Mary had her first heart attack less than three months after I was fired—and you wonder. A cruel man and a cruel fate intervene and change your life.[24]

But still unchastened, Iacocca began again at Chrysler, expecting to work his usual sales and promotion magic.

> I was . . . confident of my own abilities. I knew the car business, and I knew I was good at it. In my heart I honestly believed that the place would be humming within a couple of years.[25]

He built a talented and experienced executive team, hired the best advertising talent, cut costs but learned that Chrysler's problems were basic ones of production and financial control. Just when these were close to being resolved, the fates struck again. The fall of the shah of Iran and the militancy of the new Iranian regime triggered the energy crisis of the early 1970s, followed by the deep recession and high interest rates of the late 1970s.

Chrysler had to raise capital to revamp its production facilities while its sales revenues were plummeting and its credit was already overextended. Faced with bankruptcy, Iacocca had to become a salesman to Congress and the Carter administration for the loan guarantees that made raising the capital feasible. In so doing he found himself stigmatized by his business colleagues as a believer in government bailouts of inefficient enterprises. In defending himself Iacocca had to admit that there were some competitive forces and economic circumstances in the face of which individual effort could not succeed without government backing. Even with the loan guarantees from the U.S. Treasury, high interest rates drained off cash, so that by late 1981 Chrysler was staying in business through the support of its big suppliers. These behind-the-scenes supports made the 1983 comeback possible, though in the public eye it was Iacocca's face on the TV advertisements for Chrysler products that heralded the recovery.

He relished the public adulation but in moments of reflection had to admit that he couldn't have succeeded alone. Nonetheless, he concludes his memoir with a set of policy statements that sound like the beginning of a run for nomination as a presidential candidate. This marketing genius feels cheated when impersonal economic or political forces undermine his agency, and the last chapters suggest that he still believes *next time* he'll reach his objective unscathed.

Work figures in a totally different way in the memoir by James D. Watson (b. 1928) of the two-year period in the early 1950s when he and Francis Crick discovered the structure of the DNA molecule. In *The Double Helix: A Personal Account of the Discovery of the Structure of DNA*, Watson describes the roles of personalities, cultural traditions, friendship, erotic drives, food, drink and travel as they played upon his inner monologue and upon discussions with colleagues about the puzzle of DNA, which had preoccupied him since his undergraduate days.

With much humor and more frankness, he describes his encounters with the European network of scientists concerned with genetics and the emerging field of molecular biology. His dislike for the Scandinavian winter and his mentor's divorce took him from a laboratory in Copenhagen to Naples and its renowned Zoological Station, to a scientific conference where he met for the first time Maurice Wilkins, the British biophysicist who had begun to study the structure of DNA by X-ray diffraction. From Wilkins he learned that DNA's stucture might be crystalline, and immediately his interest was aroused. A random decision to stop off in Geneva on his way back from Naples put him in touch with a colleague who had been working at Cal Tech and had heard the famed Linus Pauling claim to have discovered the helical structure of proteins.

Now the pace of Watson's narrative quickens because he instantly understood that Pauling might beat him to the structure of DNA and preempt the field in which Watson wanted to build his career.

The search for a setting in which he could pursue his interest among colleagues who could teach him about X-ray diffraction and structural analysis took him to Cambridge, where the mood and personal relationships were highly congenial.

> *From my first day in the lab I knew I would not leave Cambridge for a long time. Departing would be idiocy for I had immediately discovered the fun of talking to Francis Crick. Finding someone in Max's [Max Perutz, his formal mentor at Cambridge] lab who knew that DNA was more important than proteins was real luck. Moreover, it was a great relief to me not to spend full time learning X-ray analysis of proteins. Our lunch conversations quickly centered on how genes were put together. Within a few days after my arrival, we knew what to do: imitate Linus Pauling and beat him at his own game.*[26]

A complex web of intersections among Watson; his partner, Crick; their rivals in Great Britain, Maurice Wilkins and Rosalind Franklin at Kings College, University of London; the mistaken formulation of another crystallographer of the theory for the diffraction of X rays by helical molecules and the unwitting collaboration of the U.S. Department of State in preventing Linus Pauling from attending a scientific conference in London combined to enable Watson and Crick to solve the puzzle first, thereby launching modern genetics and earning them the Nobel Prize.

In Watson's narrative, all is contingent. He depicts himself as a youthful midwesterner, in flight along with his sister from the social and intellectual dullness of Middle America. The behavior of those from whom he was supposed to learn was erratic, as much influenced by factors like his Copenhagen supervisor's divorce as by scientific curiosity. His life outside the laboratory was consumed by the unfulfilled quest to find someplace warm in Cambridge where the food would not foster a developing ulcer, and by the equally unfulfilled quest to find beautiful and sexy female companions. Much advice given him was useless, while he was hampered by his inability or unwillingness to learn the chemistry he needed to come up with the answers he was seeking.

Yet these multiple causes all work out to the dazzling conclusion. Watson and Crick had been held up in their work by the slowness of the lab's machinist in preparing the materials for model building. But at last the moment arrived.

> *Only a little encouragement was needed to get the final soldering accomplished in the next couple of hours. The brightly shining metal plates were then immediately used to make a model in which for the first time all the DNA components were present. In about an hour I had arranged the atoms in positions which satisfied both the X-ray data and the laws of stereochemistry. The resulting helix was right-handed with the two chains running in opposite directions. Only one person can easily play with a model, and so Francis did not try to check my work until I backed away and said that I thought everything fitted.*[27]

We meet a new type of hero in this narrative—one who bobs about on the sea of large, impersonal causal forces, and from time to time, through serendipity, his intellect seizes the moment which makes him himself, a cause—acting on others instead of being acted upon. This we may take for the midtwentieth-century sense of agency—which governs until the effort to deconstruct the individual and the single narrative point of view takes hold in the 1980s. Watson's story also underlines the extent to which modern ease of travel and intellectual networks transform the sensibility of an otherwise quintessentially American narrator.

CHAPTER THREE

THE ROMANTIC HEROINE

THE ROMANTIC HEROINE emerged in the late eighteenth century as the archetypal female figure in modern European culture. Romantic writers like Rousseau and Coleridge made the female heroine's sexual powers both dangerous and unpredictable, mirroring the spontaneity of nature. But they also made her essentially passive, someone acted upon rather than her own agent. As an erotic being whose sensuality was very much of this world, and whose intellect was of minor importance, she stood in sharp contrast to the medieval and early modern woman spiritual figure, who sublimated her sexuality in the search for a closer union with God and was capable of learned comment on theology.

As described first by Rousseau and then by all the principal male figures in the romantic movement, the romantic female's sexuality existed to be subsumed within that of her male partner. This fundamentally male projection on the female figure was so firmly established in literary culture by the early nineteenth century that it began to shape women's narratives. Women romantic writers like Margaret Fuller in America and George Sand in France made the romantic female a more active figure through the use of her intuition and her power to see into the heart of things, but they too acquiesced in defining her as closer to nature than men.

After the rise of feminism in the 1840s, the romantic heroine's place was contested by women artists, professionals and cultural rebels, new social types who were seeking to achieve on their own.

Such feminist women got bad press from male writers, who were busy inventing the kind of heroine suited to being the complement of the male romantic sensibility.

In the long run, the romantic life plot became the *ur* narrative for women in both popular and learned culture in Europe and North America, because it fit with the major economic and demographic forces shaping modern bourgeois society. As the nineteenth century unfolded, the shift from religious to secular worldviews meant that the locus of emotional life was moving from church to family, so there were good cultural reasons for seeing the telos of a woman's life in marriage and domesticity.

In the late eighteenth and early nineteenth centuries, the focus of Protestant emotional life became the family as much as church or chapel. Because of Protestant belief in the necessity of a conversion experience before acceptance into full membership in the church, the home became the setting for producing youthful conversions. Anglicans and Catholics might have the baby baptized and count it a member of the faith from infancy, but because it was the responsibility of parents to ensure their children's conversion, the Protestant household needed to exclude all experiences which were contrary to the development of faith. As worship at home became increasingly important, a mother's moral instruction of young children became not just a matter of inculcating manners and deportment but a path to salvation.

At the same time the development of the factory system of production removed much economic activity from the household, permitting the middle class to relocate domestic life in suburbs, where children would be free from the health dangers of unsanitary cities and removed from the influence of rowdy and unlettered apprentices and journeymen. Along with this physical relocation came the first efforts of the bourgeois to limit family size, thereby, in the absence of effective birth control, focusing more attention on controlling or managing sexual passion. The notion of a maternal figure as "the angel of the house" thus replaced the picture of the female as a competent economic and sexual partner, and permitted the separation of women into idealized maternal figures or déclassé women of overt sexuality and easy virtue.

Thus the life plot for the female developed a form seen in the great nineteenth-century novels and in opera in which the telos of

a woman's life is her meeting and potential union with the appropriate male romantic partner, and the dynamics of the action come
from the efforts of scheming relatives, class conventions, wicked
tyrants and other forces of destiny to keep the true lovers apart.
One of the complementary plot conventions of nineteenth-century
opera is the story of the tenderhearted woman of the demimonde,
like Violetta in *La Traviata*, who surrenders her lover so that he can
marry a "pure" young woman and establish a suitably respectable
family.

In the novels of Jane Austen and George Eliot we see a satiri-
cal female eye cast upon this basic plot and its depiction of
women, but the major male writers of the era were its enthusiastic
proponents. So the romantic heroine inexorably takes center stage
as a harmonious female representation of the economic, social and
emotional forces requiring expression through the gender system.
For we may understand gender categories as symbolic expressions
of social, economic and erotic realities.

Not surprisingly, the emergence of a tradition of female autobiography in modern Europe and its offshoots provides many
counternarratives to the romantic female plot, but by the midnineteenth century even the most subversive female lives were
being crammed into romantic form, reflecting the degree to which
culture and social structures required this construction of female
experience. If we trace the stages by which this remarkable uniformity came about, we see that it was most striking in urban cultural
centers and weakest on the margins of society.

In North America the conditions of settlement, and frontier
warfare with Indian tribes being driven from traditional hunting
grounds, produced a unique seventeenth- and eighteenth-century
form of women's memoir in the widely read narratives of captivity,
when women were taken hostage by Indians and forced to live the
life of supposedly "savage" people.

Such stories were riveting for readers in North America and
Europe, because their narrators were seen as reporting on experiences which challenged social and racial hierarchies. Further,
women captives could be seen as experiencing sexuality in ways
outside the cultural controls of Western Europe society, a subject
charged with erotic meaning. Since Indians normally scalped adult
male prisoners, the captives who returned were mainly women.

These survivors could speak and write with an authorial voice not usually available to European women.

By the nineteenth century, as the Abolition movement grew in strength in England and North America, the stories of black women slaves who escaped to freedom claimed similar authority. Theirs was an experience no one else could report. Their lives under slavery also challenged categories of race, class and sexuality, since they had been forcibly subject to white sexual exploitation. They could also expose Western sentimentality about maternity, because they had seen their children taken from them and subjected to slavery.

Nonetheless, by the midnineteenth century the romantic pattern had been superimposed on such stories, so that we can speak of a tradition in women's writing which conceals agency, concentrates on inner life and leaves women pretty much disembodied, since the dictates of sexual propriety and of romanticism did not permit women to speak about physical experience. Such uniformity, so easily contrasted with the decisive patterns of action laid out in male memoirs, has prompted some critics to claim the existence of a separate female genre of autobiography, a genre concerned exclusively with interior life as opposed to male action.

To make such a claim is to confuse the effects of social location and cultural conditioning upon women's experience and to assume, needlessly, a biological imperative to express one's life through interior sensation rather than external action. Since the image of the female in any culture is never separate, but always paired with that of the male, it is not surprising that women have come up with life histories which seem complementary to those of men. Certainly they have responded to the romantic convention of the passive female by concealing the springs of action in their lives. The complex interplay of economic, emotional and demographic forces with understandings of gender also foster a common narrative approach for women writers, since they are both products and chroniclers of the cultural conventions to which they conform, even in the act of writing.

To understand the effects of social location we need only look at the female sensibilities revealed in the memoirs of two seventeenth-century women, Mary Rowlandson (1635–1678), a famous Indian captive, and her nearly exact contemporary, Margaret

Cavendish (1623–1673), Duchess of Newcastle. Both women faced danger, and hardship from the fortunes of war, but Rowlandson became the captive of Indians during the conflict between the American settlers in Massachusetts and the French, and their Indian allies. Margaret Cavendish faced danger through her own and her husband's loyalty to the Stuart monarchs in the English Civil War. She was willing to risk imprisonment by returning to England to try to salvage some part of the family's estates while her husband was in exile, but she describes herself as frightened at trifles and lacking the capacity to defend herself.

Mary Rowlandson, in her *Sovereignty and Goodness of God, Together with the Faithfulness of His Promises Displayed* (1682), could always explain her courage in extreme psychological and physical suffering as provided by divine grace. Her memoir shows her alone on the fourth stage of her forced journey with her Indian captors, suffering from exposure and starvation in the cold of deep winter. As she reflects on her situation, she is refreshed by her Bible.

> *Heart-aking thoughts here I had about my poor Children, who were scattered up and down among the wild beasts of the forrest: My head was light and dissey (either through hunger or hard lodging, or trouble or altogether) my knees feeble, my body raw by sitting double night and day, that I cannot express to man that affliction that lay upon my Spirit, but the Lord helped me at that time to express it to himself. I opened my Bible to read, and the Lord brought that precios Scripture to me, Jer. 31. 16.* Thus saith the Lord, refrain thy voice from weeping, and thine eyes from tears, for thy work shall be rewarded, and they shall come again from the land of the Enemy. *This was sweet cordial to me when I was ready to faint.* [1]

Margaret Cavendish felt obliged to maintain the standard female character while describing her efforts for her husband's well-being.

> *In some cases I am naturally a coward, and in other cases very valiant; as, for example, if any of my nearest friends were in danger, I should never consider my life in striving to help them, though I were sure to do them no good, and would will-*

ingly, nay cheerfully, resign my life for their sakes; likewise I should not spare my Life if honor bids me die; but in danger where my Friends or my Honor is not concerned, or engaged, but only my Life to be unprofitably lost, I am the veriest coward in Nature, as upon the Sea, or any dangerous places, or of Thieves, or fire, or the like; Nay, the shooting of a gun, although but a Pot-gun, will make me start, and stop my hearing, much less have I courage to discharge one.[2]

Rachel Plummer (d. 1839), captured by Comanches in Texas in 1836, also watched her family dispersed among Indian captors. Pregnant at the time of her capture, she was forced to watch her newborn infant killed brutally before her eyes by her Comanche masters, who thought the baby would decrease her capacity to work. Eventually, she became so despairing at her circumstances that she began to resist her captors, hoping to be killed. Her language describing her resistance is as terse as that of any male account of a fight.

My young mistress and myself were out a short distance from town. She ordered me to go back to town and get a kind of instrument with which they dig roots. Having lived as long, and indeed longer, than life was desirable, I determined to aggravate them to kill me. I told her I would not go back. She, in an enraged tone, bade me go. I told her I would not. She then with savage screams ran at me. I knocked, or, rather, pushed her down. She, fighting and screaming like a desperado, tried to get up; but I kept her down: and in the fight I got hold of a large buffalo bone. I beat her over the head with it, although expecting at every moment to feel a spear reach my heart from one of the Indians; but I lost no time. I was determined if they killed me, to make a cripple of her. . . . No one touched me. I had her past hurting me, and indeed, nearly past breathing, when she cried out for mercy. . . . She was bleeding freely; for I had cut her head in several places to the skull. I raised her up and carried her to the camp.[3]

It helped, Plummer comments, that she now "took my own part, and fared much better by it." Plummer is reporting a fight for physical and psychological survival in the flat, unvarnished language of frontier Texas. She had been living in a world beyond the reach of romantic convention, and it shows in her language.

Anna Cora Mowatt (1819–1870), located in affluent New York society, describing events in the same decade as Plummer's captivity, had to clothe her resolve to "take my own part" in different language.

Mowatt was the youthful bride of a successful lawyer whose fortune and ability to practice his profession vanished because of illness and unsuccessful speculation. On learning that they were penniless, and that all their possessions had to be sold to settle debts, Mowatt decided to earn the family living. But, because romanticism shaped the New York literary scene of which she was part, the decision required some careful emotional dressing up.

> *Misfortune sprinkles ashes on the head of the man, but falls like dew on the heart of the woman, and brings forth germs of strength of which she herself had no conscious possession.*
>
> *That afternoon I walked alone for a long time in the lovely arbor that had been erected for my pleasure. . . . I thought of my eldest sister, Charlotte. Her gift was for miniature painting. When the rude storms of adversity had shipwrecked her husband, she had braved the opposition of her friends, of the world, and converted what had been a mere accomplishment into the means of support for herself and her children. . . . Were there no gracious gifts within my nature? Had I no talents I could use? Had a life made up of delightful associations and poetic enjoyments unfitted me for exertion? No—there was something strong within me that cried out, It had not!*[4]

Mowatt here presents herself as drawing on unconscious strength to gain the courage to defy convention and earn her living.

> *I could give public readings. I had often read before large assemblages of friends—that required not a little courage. With a high object in view, I should gain enough additional courage to read before strangers.*[5]

Her narrative, unlike Plummer's, is replete with standard romantic images. Mowatt is shown close to nature, calling upon powers of which she is not conscious. Her heart, not her intellect, was the source of her decision to act courageously, not on her own behalf but on behalf of others. What Mowatt was in fact doing was reaching a rational decision about a course of action which she intended to pursue despite the social sanctions against it. We cannot know whether Mowatt was consciously manipulating romantic categories to make her reported actions more acceptable to her readers or whether she saw herself through the mirror of internalized romantic imagery. What we can see is how complicated romantic categories make women's reporting of decisive action.

The most striking later-nineteenth-century female narratives which report decisive action with clarity come from slave women, who could never internalize romantic self-imagery because they were never offered male protection and because slavery never permitted recognition that men and women could form abiding emotional bonds. Black women's sexuality was exploited by white males without the slightest pretense of affection, and their children were callously consigned to slavery regardless of the white culture's sentimental view of maternity. So Harriet Jacobs (1813–1897) could write a brisk, fast-moving narrative about her flight to freedom, in which she is clearly the rational agent of her escape. Once she had fled a tyrannical and cruel owner, Dr. Flint, Jacobs, safe in concealment, exulted over her first victory over him.

> *Opposite my window was a pile of feather beds. On the top of these I could lie perfectly concealed, and command a view of the street through which Dr. Flint passed to his office. Anxious as I was, I felt a gleam of satisfaction when I saw him. Thus far I had outwitted him, and I triumphed over it.*[6]

Jacobs concludes her narrative by stressing its difference from the contemporary romantic view of a female life.

> *Reader, my story ends with freedom; not in the usual way, with marriage. I and my children are now free! We are as free from the power of slaveholders as are the white people of the north;*

and though that, according to my ideas, is not saying a great deal, it is a vast improvement in my condition.[7]

The experience of the leading women reformers of the Progressive era gave rise to a remarkable outburst of memoir writing by educated white American women. They were in the first American generation to gain access to graduate education and the pioneers of women's professions like nursing and social work. Unlike Jacobs, who points out to the reader that romantic categories don't apply to her, these lifelong activists represent themselves as larger than life maternal figures, to whom involvement in important social causes just happened.

The most popular of these narratives, by Jane Addams (1860–1935), *Twenty Years at Hull-House* (1910) describes Addams's childhood, education and the launching of her career as a social reformer in the raw immigrant city of Chicago in the late 1880s. No language could be more deceptive than Addams's about the manner in which she came to found one of America's earliest settlement houses.

It is hard to tell just when the very simple plan which afterward developed into the Settlement began to form itself in my mind. It may have been before I went to Europe for the second time, but I gradually became convinced that it would be a good thing to rent a house in a part of the city where many primitive and actual needs are found, in which young women who have been given over too exclusively to study, might restore a balance of activity along traditional lines and learn from life itself.[8]

Actually Addams's letters reveal that she had developed a written plan, entitled "the scheme," which she had drawn up in Europe in 1887 after several years of careful study of European communitarian life and urban social reform. She had visited Benedictine and Ursuline communities of women, studied the utopian communities formed outside Paris following the Paris Commune and stayed in London's Toynbee Hall, where a community of young university men, dons and students, took up residence to try to contribute some benefit from their education to the lives of the poor in the East End of London. Her diary, which she had before her as she wrote her memoir, records the exact dates of many of the events which prepared the way for launching the project. Moreover Addams kept a copy of "the scheme" among her papers.

Yet she writes about the decision to launch her new and innovative institution using language which is studiously in the passive voice. She talks about the plan "beginning to form itself in my mind." Here she is using words that suggest inspiration from some external source rather than rational reflection and decision. In fact, when she launched Hull-House in 1889 she translated every element of her 1887 scheme into action.

Addams even makes the experience which first interested her in the urban poor seem to have occurred without any volition on her part. She reports that on her first visit to London, in 1883, she was one of a small party of tourists who

> were taken to the East End by a city missionary to witness the Saturday night sale of decaying vegetables and fruit, which, owing to the Sunday laws in London, could not be sold until Monday, and, as they were beyond safekeeping, were disposed of at auction as late as possible on Saturday night.[9]

Here Addams represents herself as being "taken" to what she describes as the most formative experience along her path to becoming committed to a lifetime of social reform. But from her travel diaries it is clear that Addams requested the trip and kept prodding the city missionary to take her to the experience she describes as a revelation sent to her by destiny.

Through her extensive use of conditional tenses and the passive voice, Addams is able to conceal her own role in making the events of her life happen and to conform herself to the romantic image of the female, seeming to be all emotion and spontaneity, and to be shaped by circumstances beyond her control. Once we grasp her skill in doing this we have learned an important point about later-nineteenth- and early-twentieth-century women's autobiography. We can be sure that whenever women autobiographers are hiding behind the passive voice and the conditional tense, they are depicting events in which they acted forthrightly upon a pre-conceived, rational plan.

Of course, in modern romantic culture planning is a sign of foresight in a man and is called scheming when practiced by women. This pejorative distinction raises the question of whether Addams and her generation knew what they were doing, or whether they had simply internalized a code that required such self-presentation. This is an important question because the continued operation of an internalized code would explain why, almost a century later, women professionals still find it hard to claim their victories and to celebrate their achievements. It is possible that Addams and her generation believed that they had to present themselves in the approved romantic way in order to secure wide-spread support for their programs of social reform. Only if they fit the proper maternal picture could they call out popular backing for child welfare and for labor laws protecting women workers, and humane concern for the unemployed, which were their principal causes in life.

There are certainly clues about some of the adolescent perceptions that were integrated into Addams's adult identity. As a child she was deeply impressed by her father's revered political associate in Illinois Abraham Lincoln. After Lincoln's assassination Addams posed a series of questions in her diary that added up to asking herself what *she* would do that carried on the tradition of the Great Emancipator. And during her early days at Rockford Female Seminary (soon to be Rockford College), she wrote home to her older sister describing her discovery that she seemed "born to run things." In other words, she had from childhood identified herself as a leader and had discovered early that people followed her. As an adult she wrote to friends briskly and authoritatively about their shared goals and objectives, in a voice which is almost the complete opposite of the woman presented in her memoir.

Only once does her actual role as the leader and principal fund-raiser for Hull-House, and voluntary welfare agent for the unemployed in the city of Chicago, appear in *Twenty Years at Hull-House*, and then only indirectly. Addams lets the mask slip, seemingly by accident, to reveal herself as a busy manager of people. Describing her perplexity and moral unease at living comfortably among people suffering profound poverty, Addams recounts a visit she and a friend paid to Tolstoy. The famous Russian novelist, sage and hero of the nineteenth-century movement to identify with the rural peasantry was a hero for late-nineteenth-century social reformers, and Addams was no exception. Tolstoy's life in rural Russia provided clarity about how one went about mixing one's labor with the peasantry, but Addams reports that she went away puzzling about how to follow the same discipline in Chicago.

> I read everything of Tolstoy's that had been translated into English, German or French [and] there grew up in my mind a conviction that what I ought to do on my return to Hull-House, was to spend at least two hours every morning in the little bakery which we had recently added to the equipment of our coffeehouse. Two hours work would be but a wretched compromise, but it was hard to see how I could take more time out of each day. . . . I did not quite see how my activity would fit in with that of the German union baker who presided over the Hull-House bakery, but all such matters were secondary and certainly could be arranged. . . . I held fast to the belief that I should do this, through the entire journey homeward, on land and sea, until I actually arrived in Chicago when suddenly the whole scheme seemed to me as utterly preposterous as it doubtless was. The half dozen people invariably waiting to see me after breakfast, the piles of letters to be opened and answered, the demand of actual and pressing human wants,—were all these to be pushed aside and asked to wait while I saved my soul by two hours work at baking bread?[10]

The list of appointments, the correspondence to be dealt with, the pressing human needs for which money had to be raised—all are the characteristic tasks of a busy administrator and builder of an institution. They slip into the narrative because Addams is concentrating on the humor inherent in the clash of cultures between rural Russia and urban Chicago, the union baker at Hull-House and the Russian serfs still bound to the land. She never shows herself actually *doing* the tasks she describes, but the simple list identifies how she spent her day, managing people, public policy and money. It is revealing that the list appears in a comic passage, where the joke is on Addams herself, so that her daily activities are made to seem vaguely comic.

Addams was not alone in concealing her own agency. Margaret Sanger (1879–1966), the determined and unshakable sexual radical who succeeded in building a popular birth-control movement in the United States, presents herself in a similar fashion in *Margaret Sanger: An Autobiography* (1938). Sanger believed that her mother's early death from tuberculosis had been brought on by repeated pregnancies, and she took up a nursing career, as the next best thing to studying medicine, so that she could work at a calling concerned with women's health. As a young mother in New York just after the turn of the century, she could not take up general nursing because of the unpredictable time demands of her family, but she could work as an obstetric nurse, knowing when she would be needed for a delivery and how long her stay away from her children might be.

Her papers record that she worked diligently to publicize her services, and that she was especially attracted to working in the poorer areas of the city, because that was where her services mattered most. But in her memoir she describes her work as being shaped by a destiny beyond her control.

> During these years in New York, trained nurses were in great demand. Few people wanted to enter hospitals for fear of being "practised" upon. . . . Sentiment was especially vehement in the matter of having babies. A woman's own bedroom, no matter how inconveniently arranged, was the usual place for her lying-in. I was not sufficiently free from domestic duties to be a general nurse, but I could ordinarily manage obstetrical cases because I was notified far enough ahead to plan my schedule. And after serving my two weeks I could get home again.
>
> Sometimes I was summoned to small apartments occupied by young clerks, insurance salesmen, or lawyers, just starting out, most of them under thirty and whose wives were having their first or second baby. . . .
>
> But more and more my calls began to come from the Lower East Side, as though I were being magnetically drawn there by some force outside my control. I hated the wretchedness and

hopelessness of the poor, and never experienced that satisfaction
in working with them that many noble women have found. My
concern for my patients was now quite different from my earlier
hospital attitude. I could see that much was wrong with them
that did not appear in the physiological or medical diagnosis. A
woman in childbirth was not merely a woman in childbirth. My
expanded outlook included a view of her background, her po-
tentialities as a human being, the kind of children she was bear-
ing and what was going to happen to them.[11]

Although we know Sanger's summonses came because she
worked hard at publicizing her services, she presents her calls to
the Lower East Side, New York's poorest immigrant quarter, as
something that just happened to her. By describing herself as
"being magnetically drawn there" by fates that were "outside my
control," Sanger manages to suggest to the reader that her vocation
came to her from somewhere beyond her own consciousness and
volition.

There follows the inevitable scene at which Sanger attends the
deathbed of a woman dying from a botched abortion, a pathetic
figure who previously begged Sanger for advice about birth control.
Sanger describes herself as not wanting to answer this particular
call.

For a wild moment I thought of sending someone else . . . but I
hurried into my uniform, caught up my bag and started out. All
the way I longed for a subway wreck, an explosion, anything to
keep me from having to enter that home again. But nothing
happened, even to delay me.[12]

After the inevitable death scene she says she hoped the fates
would preserve her from witnessing, Sanger returned home close
to dawn. Gazing out her window at the darkened city, she recognized her calling.

I looked out my window and down upon the dimly lighted city.
Its pains and griefs crowded in upon me, a moving picture
rolled before my eyes with photographic clearness: women
writhing in travail to bring forth little babies; the babies them-

selves naked and hungry, wrapped in newspapers to keep them from the cold; six-year-old children with pinched, pale, and wrinkled faces, old in concentrated wretchedness, pushed into grey and fetid cellars.[13]

When the sun rose, it was the dawn of a new day for Sanger, because she now accepted the calling which she describes as unsought and thrust upon her by fate. Thereafter, she does describe herself acting decisively, but now she sees herself not as working on her own behalf but as an agent of a cause, for which she has been chosen.

In real life, Sanger was a much more dramatic sexual radical than her memoir suggests, and she was an able strategist and tactician in radical causes. But her autobiography was written to advance the birth-control cause, and a full-dress presentation as a romantic heroine was one sure way to ensure enthusiastic readers.

Ellen Glasgow (1873–1945), an exact contemporary of Sanger's and a highly successful novelist, whose work depicts the cultural tensions between Old and New South, shows us the full-fledged romantic heroine, depicted in her memoir with all the skill of a polished writer. Glasgow's mother was from the old tidewater aristocracy, while her father represented the new industrial South, something Glasgow both despised and found attractive for its raw energy.

Made shy by deafness as a young woman, Glasgow nonetheless used her earnings as a successful novelist to escape from Richmond to New York, where she and her sister went twice a year. There she seemed to hear a little better, and was even able to enjoy going into society. Thus we have our heroine, gifted, sadly isolated by deafness, physically beautiful—and the inevitable happens.

Without warning, a miracle changed my life. I fell in love at first sight. . . . Loneliness had exercised a strong fascination; and I felt that I could not surrender myself to constant companionship, that I could not ever be completely possessed.[14]

But, of course Glasgow, like many brilliant and highly educated women, fell first for a married man, so the commitment could be easily managed. The presentation of the moment is worthy of grand opera, so that we almost expect the chapter to close with a great love duet.

> *Like all other romantic episodes, great or small, in my life, this began with a sudden illumination. . . . One moment the world had appeared in stark outlines, colorless and unlit, and the next moment it was flooded with radiance. I had caught the light from the glance of a stranger, and the smothered fire had flamed up from the depths. . . .*
>
> *I felt my gaze drawn back to him by some invisible thread of self-consciousness. I was aware of his interest, and I was aware, too, of his tall, thin figure and his dark keen face, with hair that was slightly gray on the temples. What I did not know at the time, for his name meant nothing to me, was that he had been married for years, and was the father of two sons, already at school or at college. What I knew, through some vivid perception, was that the awareness was not on my side alone, that he was following my words and my gestures, that a circle of attraction divided us from those around us. . . . In the years before my life was clouded by tragedy, I had known an attraction as swift and as imperative, but not ever the permanence, and the infallible certainty, as if a bell were ringing, "here, now, this is my moment!"[15]*

Glasgow, outwardly the genteel Southern lady, had a seven-year secret affair with her romantic hero. But such happiness could not last, and she learned of his death from a newspaper, just after they had spent a happy interlude together in Switzerland.

Reflecting on her life at the close of her autobiography (written late in life and published shortly after her death), Glasgow acknowledges that she had lived an unconventional life, and done exactly what she chose, but her freedom had remained secret, a private world behind the mask of conformity.

> *Only on the surface of things have I ever trod the beaten path. So long as I could keep from hurting anyone else, I have lived, as completely as it were possible, the life of my choice. I have been free.[16]*

Living the life of one's choice while publicly conforming to the expected female role, and daring to tell about the secret life only on the eve of one's death, suggests a life lived holding extreme contradictions in somewhat shaky balance. Glasgow may be the pure exponent of the romantic heroine in her self-reporting, but in fact Glasgow the independent female of means, who supported herself in considerable style by her earnings as a novelist, keeps popping up in the syntax of Glasgow's finely chiseled prose.

> *I bought the smartest hats from Paris, and, as my books were bringing in a little money, I went, for my clothes, to fashionable dressmakers. . . .*
>
> *Whether it was the gay clothes or the demolished inhibitions, I do not know; but that spring, for the first time, I felt that it was possible to overcome what I had regarded as an insurmountable impediment. . . . I will make myself well, I resolved. I will make myself happy, I will make myself beautiful.* [17]

These assertions of the will show us the romantic female briskly taking charge of the fates, even if only to make herself more appealingly romantic.

In the 1960s educated American women abandoned the romantic myth in droves after reading Betty Friedan's *Feminine Mystique* (1963) or Shulamith Firestone's *Dialectic of Sex* (1970). Their British and European sisters were not far behind them, many looking back with deep sadness, or a mixture of rage and sorrow, at what maintaining the romantic facade had cost their mothers and, through them, their daughters. One of the most moving descriptions of that changed worldview was written by Gloria Steinem (b. 1934) in "Ruth's Song (Because She Could Not Sing It)" (1983).

Steinem's mother lost her mind and lived the life of an oversedated, desperate, barely functioning housewife throughout her younger daughter's childhood. Steinem, taking on the attitudes of other family members, at first believed her mother's mental illness to be something hereditary and never questioned why she was so disturbed and always in need of the bottle of chloral hydrate she carried everywhere.

But then Steinem began to ask questions. She learned that her mother had once been brisk, competent, ambitious and very much in charge of herself.

> She had been a spirited, adventurous young woman, who strug-
> gled out of a working class family and into college, who found
> work she loved and continued to do, even after she was married
> and my older sister was there to be cared for. . . . She was thirty
> before she gave up her own career to help my father run the
> Michigan summer resort that was the most practical of his many
> dreams, and she worked hard there at everything from book-
> keeper to bar manager. The family must have watched this ener-
> getic, fun-loving, book-loving woman turn into someone who
> was afraid to be alone, who could not hang onto reality long
> enough to hold a job, and who could rarely concentrate enough
> to read a book.[18]

Steinem sees her mother's marriage in decidedly unromantic terms as a dead end, in which she was trapped by an unrealistic attachment to a man incapable of supporting her. The loss of her work, the disillusionment of poverty, the loneliness of the summer resort in which she was finally abandoned are the reality of what happened to her mother, and there is not the slightest hint of anything romantic about it.

In *Fierce Attachments* (1987) Vivian Gornick (b. 1935) tells the story of her parents' marriage with a mixture of humor and rage which keeps swinging between the comic dimensions of her parents' ill-suited relationship and the suffering inflicted on the Gornick children when their father died, and their mother insisted on playing the part of the bereaved romantic heroine.

> She had made such an intolerable romance of her marriage, had
> impaled us all on the cross of my father's early death. . . . Love,
> she said, was everything. A woman's life was determined by love.
> All evidence to the contrary—and such evidence was abundant
> indeed—was consistently discounted and ignored, blotted out of
> her discourse, refused admission by her intellect.[19]

Gornick's rage was focused on the degree to which her mother made herself a totally negative romantic heroine, so thoroughly engrossed in her performance as bereaved widow that her children had no place in her life, except as a suitable backdrop to the star performer.

> *Widowhood provided Mama with a higher form of being. In re-fusing to recover from my father's death she had discovered that her life was endowed with a seriousness her years in the kitchen had denied her. She remained devoted to this seriousness for thirty years. She never tired of it, never grew bored or restless in its company, found new ways to keep alive the interest it deserved and had so undeniably earned. A woman-who-has-lost-the-love-of-her-life was now her orthodoxy. She paid it Tal-mudic attention.*[20]

Gornick's memoir has as one theme the way the supposedly passive romantic heroine seeks power through the manipulation of others, especially the manipulation of her children through guilt. Gornick makes the reader feel the suffocating mood in the family's small apartment, how she dreaded her mother's return from work, longed to flee, to live with someone sane, to spread her wings and feel alive. But those desires only compounded her guilt at not shar-ing her mother's transports of sorrow.

> *On Friday I prepared myself for two solid days of weep-ing and sighing, and the mysterious reproof that depression leaks into the air like the steady escape of gas when the pilot light is extinguished. I woke up guilty and went to bed guilty, and on weekends the guilt accumulated into a low-grade infection.*[21]

Thirty years later Gornick speaks a truth her mother doesn't want to hear, during one of their scenes of mutual recrimination.

> *"Ma," I say, "you were forty-six when he died. You could have gone out into life. Other women with a lot less at their disposal did. You wanted to stay inside the idea of Papa's love. It's crazy! You've spent thirty years inside the idea of love. You could have had a life."*[22]

There could not be a more deflating treatment of the romantic heroine than Gornick's portrait of her mother, nor a more clinical dissection of the moral flaw at the center of the idea of the romantic female. We can see it in characters like Anna Cora Mowatt, galvanized to action by her husband's illness and financial failure. Mowatt could feel strong because he was weak. She was at her best when others were wounded. And Gornick's mother was like Demeter, ready to drown the world in tears so that she could hang on to her children, even if she could only keep them subject by guilt.

Women writers like Steinem and Gornick are reporting the truth about the potential female monster created by Rousseau's wish for union with an utterly compliant, childlike woman. Human beings who appear to be acted upon find secret ways of seeking power without ever acknowledging agency. And agency unacknowledged is not subject to moral constraints, as Gornick, for one, knows very well.

CHAPTER FOUR

IMPERIAL STORIES

T HE "NEW WORLD" offered a fresh canvas on which new ver-
sions of the hero and of the romantic female could be inscribed.
Western Europeans and their North American, African or Aus-
tralasian counterparts found an enlarged mode of heroic life in the
exploration and economic conquest of non-Western peoples and
the continents viewed stereotypically as "outside" the West. Some
found the new identity through conquest, others by deep identification with the "other" culture. Through their narratives the men,
at least, became icons of imperial power and models of its ideal
types, while the carefully edited female experience also sustained
cultural patterns at home.

Imperial adventures gave the narrator the exceptional experience which stimulated autobiography, just as it encouraged Aphra
Behn (1640–1685) or Joseph Conrad (1857–1924) and Rider
Haggard (1856–1925) to explore in their novels the ambiguities of
life for the European engaged in the subjugation of other cultures
and peoples. Personal narratives of missionary endeavor, of scientific expeditions and of journeys of exploration, captured major
segments of the popular reading public at home and so became an
important force shaping the archetypal male or female image as
the nineteenth century unfolded. European culture developed its
full-blown imperial form in the second half of the nineteenth century with the occupation of the African and Asian continents, and
it was from this experience that the most popular stories came.

The sponsors of exploration and cultural encounters were Catholic missionary orders, the Protestant Missionary Societies of England and the United States, and the influential British Royal Geographical Society. The interweaving of missionary activity with exploration and with scientific or political observation was so intimate that the narrators of African or Asian adventures are perpetually changing masks—at one moment reflecting on their certainty of divine guidance, at another using sextant and chronometer to assist in mapping continents and at yet another jotting down the vocabulary of native dialects like modern anthropologists.

It has been customary to consider the archetypal narratives of the exploration of Africa to have been those written by David Livingstone, Henry Morton Stanley and Richard Burton. But there is little-known but dazzling competition for this distinction in the Englishwoman Mary Kingsley, who recorded her travels in West Africa, and her successor, Gertrude Lowthian Bell, who recounted her travels in Syria.

The memoirs of many adventurous American women missionaries in Asia, along with those of their male counterparts, form an important chapter in the story of the European encounter with that continent. Moreover they were quickly disseminated to a popular readership through church newspapers and the popular lecture circuit. Emily Chubbuck Judson's *Memoir of Sarah Hall Boardman Judson of the American Mission to Burmah,* published in 1848, was a best-selling account of the life of a woman missionary of extraordinary courage, linguistic talent and administrative ability, a heroine who could safely be admired abroad while being represented at home as the quintessential redemptive female, suffering joyfully to rescue the heathen and inspire her flock. Not surprisingly, although there seems to have been little actual difference between male and female missionary roles, the ways in which women and men reported their adventures were strikingly different.

David Livingstone (1813–1873) introduced himself to the Basuto chief Sebitoane by saying that "the object of our visit [was] the preaching of the gospel, their [the Basuto's] elevation in the scale of humanity, peace and the avoidance of murder and the barter in slaves." Yet on his second visit to Sebitoane in 1852 Livingstone mused,

*If we can open up the interior to the trade of the coast and per-
suade the Makololo to take the trade of this large section of the
country into their own hands, it will be an important step in the
right direction. They will feel that the gospel is favorable to their
advancement temporally at least, and we shall be independent
of the Boers.*[1]

But even though his motives were such an obvious mix of economic, political and religious emotions, Livingstone gave thanks to
his God for the extraordinary adventure that mission work was providing in his life.

*What an unspeakable mercy to be permitted to engage in this
most honorable and holy work. What an infinity of lots in the
world are poor, miserable and degraded compared with mine.
I might have been instead of a missionary, a common soldier,
a day laborer, a factory operative or mechanic instead of a
missionary.*[2]

A settled family life mattered little for Livingstone compared
with the rewards of his work. The birth of his son, William, on
September 15, 1851, in a makeshift camp where Mrs. Livingstone
had no European helpers to attend her confinement, rated two
lines in his travel diary, along with the laconic "weather very hot."
Three days later Thomas Livingstone, aged two and a half, came
down with "river fever," a problem Livingstone noted was exacer-
bated by the 104-degree heat. Such concerns counted for little in
Livingstone's account of his work, which he estimated had resulted in 22,000 Bechuanas receiving instruction from ten European teachers aided by six native converts. The dangers of his
travels didn't worry him, because he knew that "my life is charmed
till my work is done," a belief that made his prose calm and matter-
of-fact.

His liveliest language flows for the joy of discovery. Sometime
between June and August 1851, his party came upon the river later
to be named the Zambezi. Countless Africans had seen the sight
they then celebrated, but for Livingstone it was as though he were
the first man to behold a new aspect of the Creation.

*In the afternoon we came upon the beautiful river Sesheke, and
thanked God for permitting us first to see this glorious river. All
we could say to each other was to express our great pleasure by
saying, How glorious! How magnificent! How beautiful! And
grand beyond all description it really was. Such a body of water,
at least 400 yards broad, and deep.*[3]

Naturally, because of his zest for exploration and scientific
fieldwork, there were occasions when Livingstone wondered
whether he was pursuing his missionary calling with sufficient
zeal. When the friendly chief Sebitoane, whose support had enabled Livingstone's explorations to range widely, died of a chronic
illness, Livingstone worried that he had not been zealous enough
to convert him.

*Alas! Alas! Sebitoane! I might have said more to him. God for-
give me! Free me from Blood guiltiness. If I had said more of
death I might have been suspected of having foreseen the event
and guilty of bewitching him. I might have recommended Jesus
and his great atonement more.*[4]

Sarah Hall Boardman Judson (1803–1845) traveled to Burma
in 1827 as the wife of the Baptist missionary George Boardman
and quickly established a successful mission with him in Tavoy,
several days' journey from Moulmein, among the supposedly "wild"
Karen people. At twenty-eight Sarah Boardman was widowed after
losing two of her children to tropical diseases. In her own letters
home and in church publications she was represented as remain-
ing at her post out of a sense of duty, but in fact she was a powerful
woman who carried on her husband's pattern of visiting Karen converts in remote hill villages with keen enjoyment of the adventure.
She also became administrator of a school system established by
the British which took some two hundred boarding and day students, and through private study she became an accomplished
speaker of Burmese.

At thirty-one she married the widowed Adoniram Judson, the
revered leader of the American missionaries in Burma, and for
eleven years the two were a powerful missionary team. Sarah

began to learn Talain and Peguan, two important languages for reaching new converts, while continuing her roles as administrator of the British schools for Burmese and as leader of a series of study groups for Burmese women. Judson's major work, meanwhile, was the translation of important texts into Burmese and the instruction of converts. The couple produced seven children (following Sarah's three by George Boardman) with no apparent interruption in Sarah's heavy work schedule. Moreover, she kept up an uninterrupted correspondence home, so copious that her biographer was able to chart her life using her own words.

> *When I first stood by the grave of my husband, I thought I must go home with George* [her one surviving child]. *But these poor, enquiring and Christian Karens, and the school-boys, and the Burmese Christians, would then be left without anyone to instruct them; and the poor, stupid Tavoyans would go on the road to death, with no one to warn them of their danger. How then, oh, how can I go? . . . I feel thankful that I was allowed to come to this heathen land. Oh, it is a precious privilege to tell idolaters of the Gospel; and when we see them disposed to love the Saviour, we forget all our privations and dangers.*[5]

The privations and dangers were real, but Sarah embraced them with considerable zest. On New Year's Eve in the year of her first husband's death, Sarah Boardman wrote her customary diary letter home to the *Missionary Magazine* describing her church of 110 members, made up of Karen people who came to worship by walking along jungle mountain paths over which tigers hunted and by fording alligator-filled rivers.

> *What would the Christians in New England think of travelling forty or fifty miles on foot, to hear a sermon, and beg a Christian book?*

she asked, rhetorically driving home the vitality of her converts' faith.[6]

Sarah Boardman, of course, encountered the same hazards when visiting Karen converts in remote villages, occasionally resorting to being carried over the deeper rivers but fording all those in which she could stand while her Karen companions carried the baby, George, ahead of her. On these travels she got so far from any links to Europeans that she astonished a British military party on a tiger hunt, who took her to be an apparition when she appeared with a group of followers to hold a service on the jungle path on which the hunters were also traveling.[7]

But she made no mention of this aspect of her work in her letters home, nor do her letters reveal any curiosity like Livingstone's about the flora and fauna of Burma, or about the charting of its rivers and mountains. Often she was, in fact, the first European to see some fresh natural wonder, but for her it was simply the backdrop of her work with her flock.

As gifted at acquiring language as Livingstone, Judson never mentioned the hours spent in the preparation of translations or in teaching languages to newly arrived male missionaries. She told the folks at home what fitted with their idea of Christian womanhood, adding in the components of unflinching physical courage and heroic faith to contemporary romantic ideas of women. Her correspondents were family, friends and missionary magazines, there being no American counterpart to the Royal Geographical Society which was in close touch with missionary activity. It is tempting to imagine what Judson might have reported had she had the same audience as Livingstone, but no such scientific interest was to be found in her American readers.

By the late 1860s, as the secular popular press expanded its influence through access to a newly literate mass readership, the editors of sensational newspapers began to replace missionary societies and geographers as sponsors of expeditions, so pressure mounted for ever more spectacular and bloodthirsty adventures, such as those described by Henry Morton Stanley (1841–1904) in his journey to find the missing missionary to East Africa David Livingstone, and those in his expedition to navigate the Luluaba River, from its source at Lake Tanganyika to its junction with another African river or to its mouth on the African coast.

Stanley traced the Luluaba to its link with the Congo, ending his journey at the massive Congo Delta on the West African coast. Conscious that his travels had to provide thrills for the masses in England and the United States, Stanley shifts his persona as narrator from the quiet confidence of the man or woman certain of a divine calling to the sick romanticism of the "adventure" writer. His correspondents wanted adventure and presumably were uninterested in other aspects of his travels, so Stanley gave them sensational adventure.

This description of the fight which broke out as he entered the Congo River from the Luluaba is typical of his style.

> *My blood is up. It is a murderous world, and I have begun to hate the filthy vulturous shoals who inhabit it. I pursue them up-stream, up to their villages; I skirmish in their street, drive them pell mell into the woods beyond, and level their ivory temples, with frantic haste I fire the huts, and end the scene by towing the canoes into mild stream and setting them adrift.* [8]

Stanley's journey did solve one of the major puzzles of African geography, establishing that the Luluaba flowed not to the Nile but to the Congo River. His narrative of the adventure ends with conventional pieties.

> *Grateful as I am to Him who had enabled me to pierce the Dark Continent from east to west, my heart was charged with grief, and my eyes with tears, at the thought of the many comrades and friends I had lost.* [9]

But the prayers don't ring quite true against the backdrop of unrelieved violence which Stanley describes with such élan that many contemporaries believed his accounts of his two African adventures to be wild fabrications. Certainly few men who have lived in such concentrated bloodshed for so many months as Stanley describes retain the zest for life which suffuses his narrative.

A different aura surrounds the pages of Richard Burton's accounts of his journeys to forbidden sacred places like Mecca and Harrar. Livingstone's missionary zeal and Stanley's quest of celebrity seem recognizable human motives, whereas Burton's curiosity seems eerily beyond the bounds of most quests for adventure or renown. Burton (1821–1890) thought of himself as an agent in the inevitable process of British or European conquest of Africa and Asia. As such he was in many ways insulated from the cultures he encountered. He was part spy, part diplomat, part soldier. He wrote for educated British readers, who he knew would share his relish for the great game of Empire.

On arriving in Harrar, the greatest Muslim city in Africa, which nonbelievers were expressly forbidden to visit, Burton describes an audience with the sultan in language of such quiet confidence in superiority that it makes Stanley's overheated prose sound even more inflated.

> *The guide raised a door curtain, suggested a bow, and I stood in the presence of the dreaded chief. The Amir . . . , sat in a dark room with whitewashed walls. . . . His appearance was that of a little Indian Rajah. . . . His throne was a common Indian Kursi, or raised cot about five feet long. . . . Being an invalid he rested his elbow upon a pillow, under which appeared the hilt of a Cutch sabre. Ranged in a double line, perpendicular to the Amir, stood "The court," his cousins and nearest relations with right arms bared after the fashion of Abyssinia.*[10]

Burton's description of the court and the arrangements made for his party to rest are matter-of-fact, not to say deliberately deflating of the risk he and his party faced. As the evening closed in on the night of the first European to set foot in Harrar, Burton was nothing if not cool, but he was also sensible of the drama of the moment.

> *I . . . sent a common six-barreled revolver as a present to the Amir . . . and we prepared to make ourselves as comfortable as possible. The interior of our new house was a clean room, with plain walls, and a floor of tamped earth. . . . I contrived to make . . . a bed with cushions . . . and, after seeing the mules fed and tethered, lay down to rest worn out by fatigue, and profoundly impressed with the poesie of our position. I was under the roof of a bigoted prince whose least word was death; amongst a people who detest foreigners; the only European that had ever passed over their inhospitable threshold, and the fated instrument of their future downfall.*[11]

Like Livingstone, Burton was a linguist with a sure ear for dialect and for literary form. Several months' stay in the territory later to become known as Somalia prompted careful observations on the language and literary traditions of the Somali.

> *It is strange that a dialect which has no written character should so abound in poetry and eloquence. There are thousands of songs, some local, others general upon all conceivable subjects, such as camel loading, drawing water and elephant hunting; every man of education knows a variety of them. The rhyme is imperfect being generally formed by the syllable "ay" . . . , which gives the verse a monotonous regularity; but assisted by a tolerably regular alliteration and cadence, it can never be mistaken for prose.*[12]

Burton talks like a character out of Conrad; his prose and Conrad's are examples of the intertextuality which shaped one branch of later-nineteenth-century fiction. By contrast, the female version of the imperial story never found its place in fiction, except in parody or satire. The male missionary who went native and had a lovely time with nameless aboriginal females is a standard comic character in later-nineteenth-century British drama and fiction. The happy male missionary is usually contrasted with his stuffy female companion, always described as intent on getting native women into Mother Hubbards. But women's accounts of their adventures (in which no such concerns figured) remained on the shelves of missionary society libraries, or in the hands of families and friends; they never entered popular discourse.

Nor did the writing of women explorers and scientists, whose travels were into territories every bit as dangerous as those explored by Stanley and Burton. The cultural dynamics by which their writing disappeared from the historical record have much to do with the sex of official historians and their attitudes to females but equally as much to do with what readers wanted to hear about.

Mary Kingsley (1862–1900) became an explorer and collector of the insects and fish of West Africa in her thirties, after having lived the conventional life of an upper-middle-class Englishwoman until both her parents died. Not allowed formal education, she had absorbed considerable knowledge of comparative religion from her physician-father's library and field zoology from his records of his travels. Her father's interests as a naturalist acquainted her with the works of Darwin and Huxley, which inspired her to study African religions and made her want to emulate Darwin's famous voyage on the *Beagle*.

Her account of her extensive travels in search of the Rembwé and Oguwé Rivers, carried out over eleven months in 1894 through uncharted territory between the Niger and the Congo, is a classic. Her journey took her through the territory of several warlike cannibal tribes, although Kingsley managed to become friends with all of them.

In contrast to Stanley, she traveled alone, by canoe, accompanied by only a few native crewmen. She always dressed like a Victorian lady—shirtwaist over stays, the conventional long gabardine skirt and a cap. She supported her travels and made her contacts with tribal people by trading.

> *I find I get along best by going among the unadulterated Africans in the guise of a trader; there is something reasonable about trade to all men, and you see the advantage of it is that, when you first appear among people who have never seen anything like you before, they naturally regard you as a devil: but when you want to buy or sell with them, they recognize there is something human and reasonable about you. . . .*
>
> *The trading method enables you to sit as an honored guest at far away inland village fires; it enables you to become the confidential friend of that ever powerful factor in all human societies, the old ladies. It enables you to become an associate of the con-fraternity of Witch Doctors, things being surrounded with an expedition of armed men must prevent you doing.*[13]

Unlike Stanley and Burton, Kingsley viewed herself with a comic sense of the incongruity of her role compared with what was expected of the Victorian lady, and, in so doing, she deflated rather than inflated the danger to which she was exposing herself. Consider how Stanley would have described Kingsley's experience, early in her West African adventure, of being marooned in an alligator-infested swamp.

There was a deceptive uniformity about the appearance of the rivers of West Africa, she discovered.

*Excepting the Congo, the really great river comes out to sea
with as much mystery as possible; lounging lazily along among
its mangrove swamps in a what's-it-matter-when-one-comes-out
and where's-the-hurry style, through quantities of channels
inter-communicating with each other. . . . High tide or low tide,
there is little difference in the water; the river, be it broad or
narrow, deep or shallow, looks like a pathway of polished metal;
for it is as heavy weighted with stinking mud as water can be.[14]*

In such a setting, Kingsley points out, it is easy to wander
among the mangroves absorbed in collecting specimens and become marooned at low tide. One must stop in one's lagoon until
the tide rises, she comments, surveying the surrounding crocodiles, swatting the mangrove flies and asking oneself for the thou-
sandth time why one has come to West Africa to endure the
terrible stench of the mud floating around one. On her last such
adventure, she confides,

a mighty Silurian as the Daily Telegraph *would call him, chose
to get his front paws over the stern of my canoe, and endeav-
oured to improve our acquaintance. I had to retire to the bows,
to keep the balance right, and fetch him a clip on the snout with
a paddle, when he withdrew and I paddled into the middle of
the lagoon hoping the water there was too deep for him or any of
his friends to repeat the performance.[15]*

Her first encounter with the Fan tribe, hitherto not visited by
Europeans and rumored to be savage cannibals, receives similar
treatment. Kingsley had brought with her several guides who
claimed to have friends in the first Fan village along her route to
the Rembwé River, and as the moments stretched out before the
friends could be found, the situation looked perilous.

*Never even in a picture book—have I seen such a set of wild
wicked looking savages as those we faced this night, and with
whom it was touch-and-go for twenty of the longest minutes I
have ever lived, whether we fought—for our lives I was going to
say, but it would not have been even for that, but merely for the
price of them.[16]*

At the next Fan village Kingsley visited, she was put up in the house of the headman but awakened after a few hours' sleep by the appalling stench in the hut. She tracked it to some bags hanging at one end of the room, the largest of which she opened, shaking the contents carefully into her hat. She discovered she was holding

> *a human hand, three big toes, four eyes, two ears, and other por-*
> *tions of the human frame. The hand was fresh, the others only so*
> *so, and shrivelled.*[17]

Having completed her journey through rapids, swamps filled with crocodiles, tiger-infested jungles and villages of cannibal tribes, all the while dodging tornadoes, riptides and other hazards, Kingsley settled herself into the comforts of Government House, in the pretty town of Victoria in the Cameroons, to reflect happily on her travels. There were no laments for comrades lost on the journey, because her expedition had been entirely peaceful.

> *As I sat on the verandah overlooking Victoria and the sea, in*
> *the dim soft light of the stars, with the fireflies around me, and*
> *the lights of Victoria away below, and heard the swift rush of the*
> *Lukola River, and the sound of the sea-surf on the rocks, and the*
> *tommtomming and the singing of the natives, all matching and*
> *mingling together, "Why did I come to Africa?" thought I. Why!*
> *who would not come to its twin brother hell itself for all the*
> *beauty and the charm of it?*[18]

Kingsley had a brief period of renown on her return to En-gland. Her collections of fish and insects found a place in the natural history section of the British Museum, and a number of new species were recorded with the designation *kingsleyae* to identify her as the discoverer. Her lectures on West African affairs were very popular, and her criticisms of the failures of colonial adminis-trators were to be echoed by reformers decades later. She died at age thirty-seven while nursing Boer prisoners on the Cape. And her reputation died with her. Rudyard Kipling, the master creator of the imperial legend in turn-of-the-century England, is reputed to have said of her, "Being human, she must have been afraid of something, but one never found out what it was." Being female, she had access to no institutions which could be custodians and popularizers of her exploits, so her story faded quickly, to be revived only by feminist scholars in the 1980s.

What is striking about Kingsley's self-presentation is her sense of the absurd, her refusal to accept contemporary stereotypes (the dreaded Fans seemed to her "a nice, energetic type of African") and her love of the African landscape. She retained the persona of a decidedly middle-class British lady—*I am habitually kind to animals, and besides, I do not think it ladylike to go shooting things with a gun*"[19]—but one always open to new experience, who relished risk and danger. Had she been male, she would have been the kind of figure who appeared in every schoolboy story of adventure, but her daring and unconventionality, even cloaked as they were in relentless respectability, never entered the popular model of behavior for women.

Gertrude Lowthian Bell (1868–1926) opens her account of her first travels in Syria with the comment that, for those raised in an elaborate social order, nothing equals "the exhilaration of wild travel."[20] Daughter of the holder of one of Britain's great industrial fortunes, the first woman to earn a first-class degree in modern history at Oxford, a happy escapee from "London seasons" and the requirements of a fashionable marriage, Bell developed her love for the Arab world through visits to many family members who served as British diplomats in Eastern Europe, Constantinople and Teheran.

Like many a distinguished explorer, Bell sought an alternative society where her obvious talents would be recognized, and where she could establish herself as a person of substance. Her mind and aesthetic sense were captivated by Islamic architecture and culture, so her life plan evolved out of her early travels in the Syrian desert to discover and describe some of the great architectural remains of the area.

The fact that such travels were physically arduous and often dangerous only added to the attractiveness of her project. She enjoyed eluding the corrupt and inefficient Turkish authorities and relished her entry as a privileged Englishwoman into the all-male Arab tribal world, the only part of Arab society accessible to travelers. She came not as a spy, like Burton, but as a sympathetic agent of what to her was an unquestionably superior British political culture, which she thought she could encourage to sponsor the development of an Arab state. Thus she was both the victim and the embodiment of British paternalistic attitudes, a contradiction she never understood.

I desired to write not so much a book of travel as an account of the people whom I met or who accompanied me on my way, and to show what the world is like in which they live and how it appears to them.[21]

In Bell's view, a woman could never succeed in concealing her sex, so Burton's travels disguised as an Arab were impossible for her. Instead, she let it be known that she came from a great British family and, though a friend and supporter of Arab culture, must live, even when traveling in the desert, by her own customs.

She did not claim to be the first to travel through the Syrian desert, for she had been preceded by German and American archaeological expeditions, but she believed that she represented the culture and political system which could best guide the future of the region.

Being English, I am persuaded that we are the people who could best have taken Syria in hand with the prospect of success greater than that which might be attained by a moderately reasonable Sultan.[22]

The Allied victory over Turkey in the 1914–1918 War later gave Bell her chance to take the region "in hand" politically, a process in which her knowledge of the desert tribes and their leaders was critical. But her initial impulse to explore the desert was a drive for adventure and risk, to move off the beaten path and become someone other than her circumscribed upper-class British female identity allowed.

You step forth, and, behold! the immeasurable world. The world of adventure and of enterprise, dark with hurrying storms, glittering in raw sunlight, an unanswered question and an unanswerable doubt hidden in the fold of every hill. . . . So . . . like the man in a fairy story, you feel the bands break which were

*riveted about your heart as you enter the path that stretches
across the rounded shoulder of the earth.*[23]

Her expedition set out in February 1905 with the aim of making serious studies of Roman and Byzantine ruins, and assessing
the impact of Rome and Byzantium on the Arab world. A supposedly secondary aim, which quickly overwhelmed the first, was to
study and document the way of life of the Bedouin and Druze
tribes of the desert. She traveled by horse, breaking her childhood
training and riding astride. Accompanying her was a mule train
carrying her tents, photographic equipment, such maps as were
available and a month's supply of food. Her muleteers, hired in
Lebanon, mixed the cultures of the area—two were Christian, one
a Druze, and the cook, Mikhail, was of dubious religious origin and
given to drink.

Planning to slip through the hands of the Turkish administration and head for the Druze mountains, Bell set out to find one of
the powerful tribes of the area and secure from them an escort. At
Salt, a village just beyond the Jordan Valley, Bell asked the help of
the leading merchant in solving her problem. She knew that the
Turkish guard at Amman would not give her permission to travel
the main desert road and therefore needed a guide to travel by
more remote routes. The necessary guide was produced, and Bell
continued her travels, handed on from one tribe to another, re-
maining out of reach of Turkish surveillance.

The central theme of her narrative quickly becomes the
desert, and the way of life of its migratory tribes. Bell recited Ara-
bic poetry to her guide, and whatever Arab hosts had her currently
under their protection, all gathered in a circle around the fire and
the steaming pot of bitter Arab coffee.

I looked out beyond [Gabran, her guide] *into the night and saw
the desert with his eyes, no longer empty but set thicker with associations than any city. Every line of it took on significance,
every stone was like the ghost of a hearth in which the warmth
of Arab life was hardly cold, though the fire might have been ex-
tinguished this hundred years. It was a city of shadowy outlines
visible one under the other, fleeting and changing, combining*

*into new shapes elements that were as old as Time, the new in-
distinguishable from the old, the old from the new.*[24]

Bell's imagination and sense of history made her accounts of
antiquities come alive, mingled as they were with the daily acci-
dents of travel in uncharted territory, where a misjudgment could
leave the party stranded without water. So her first encounter with
the ancient city of Khubret Hass near the village of El Barah came
on a vexing day when her coat was stolen and she and her guide
became separated from the mules and servants, wandering in
the hills for several hours after dark, cold, hungry and thirsty.
But by dawn the next day she was back again mapping the city,
photographing its wonders and sketching its major decorative
elements.

> *No words can give the charm of it nor the magic of the Syrian
> spring! The generations of the dead walk with you down the
> streets, you see them flitting across their balconies, gazing out
> windows wreathed with white clematis, wandering in palisaded
> gardens that are still planted with olive and with vine and car-
> peted with iris, hyacinth and anemone. . . . That they became
> Christian the hundreds of ruined churches and crosses carved
> over the doors and windows of their dwellings would be enough
> to show; that they were artists their decorations prove; that they
> were wealthy their spacious mansions, their summer houses and
> stables and outhouses testify. They borrowed from Greece such
> measure of cultivation and of the arts as they required, and
> fused with them the spirit of Oriental magnificence . . . ; they
> lived in comfort and security such as few of their contemporaries
> can have known, and the Mahommedan invasion swept them
> off the face of the earth.*[25]

Bell's later accounts, recording her travels in the Arabian
desert, were less successful in combining personal memoir and exploration of antiquity, mainly because her political concerns became more strident. Eventually employed as a political officer
attached to the India Expeditionary Force with the rank of major,
Bell drew the maps, provided the commentary and helped recruit

the Arab leaders who supported the Allies against the Turks in 1914–1918. Thereafter, she drew the boundaries of modern Iraq, Jordan and Syria, and advised the 1919 Peace Conference on the establishment of the Hashemite kings of Iraq and Jordan.

Her powerful political role might have ensured her place in history, and the contributions she made to the study of antiquities in Syria and Arabia ought to have ensured her scholarly reputation. But she had no political or scholarly constituency in England, since she related almost exclusively to the Foreign Office and to the Royal Geographical Society, both male institutions, which found so idiosyncratic a female troublesome. Thus, T. E. Lawrence has captured a place in history for his role with the desert tribes in 1914–1918, but the woman he failed to mention, whose research and exploration made his victories possible, has not.[26] The silence which followed Bell's death results partly from her upper-class attitudes and voice and her old worldview of geopolitics. She understood spheres of influence and paternalistic colonial relationships, but she was almost unaware of the era of Middle Eastern oil politics just dawning in the 1920s.

Imperial adventures like Bell's or Kingsley's, or the travels of Stanley or Burton, could be compellingly attractive for the individual who did not "fit in" at home. They offered excitement, real adventure and, at least for the men, the chance of earning reputation and status at home as a servant of the Empire. Skirmishes with native peoples might be dangerous, but as a bumptious Stanley reported, the odds were weighted in favor of the Europeans because of their superior weapons.

It was otherwise, however, when imperial conflicts were waged with rival European empires and the contending forces were equals in weapons and the arts of war. Then the canvas for recording imperial adventures darkened, and the agent of Empire appeared not against the bright backdrop of honor and conquest but as the existential victim in the grip of modern bureaucracy and state power. So the great conflict of 1914–1918, between rival British and German empires, led to a new presentation of the self, in which the man of war struggled to maintain his humanity in the midst of impersonal and equally inhuman bureaucratic war machines. In narratives of 1914–1918 there is little to distinguish the self-presentation of male and female—both are anguished witnesses of human folly and suffering, which they can neither alleviate nor bring to an end.

Siegfried Sassoon's account of his war experience captures the horror and irrationality of modern trench warfare and the sacrifice of thousands of lives in disputing a few hundred yards of blasted wasteland, once idyllic farmland in an almost forgotten rural France. His account of his own part in the First Battle of the Somme records the new consciousness in elegant prose. Sassoon (1886–1967) and his company had been ordered out to occupy and deepen a newly captured German trench.

> *A runner arrived with a verbal message "C Company bombers to go up at once." With a dozen men behind me I followed. . . . Darkness was giving way to unrevealing twilight as we . . . went up a shell pitted slope. It was about 500 yards across the open to the newly captured . . . trench. Just as we got there a second runner overtook us to say that my bombers were to go back again. I sent them back. I cannot say why I went on myself; but I did, and Kindle* [a youthful lance corporal from Sassoon's company] *stayed with me.*[27]

There follows an account of confused action in which Sassoon came across the body of a recently killed young German officer.

> *As I stepped over one of the Germans an impulse made me lift him up from the miserable ditch. Propped against the bank his blonde face was undisfigured, except by the mud which I wiped from his eyes and mouth with my coat sleeve. . . . He didn't look to be more than eighteen. Hoisting him a little higher, I thought what a gentle face he had. . . . Perhaps I had some dim sense of the futility which had put an end to this good-looking youth. Anyhow I hadn't expected the battle of the Somme to be quite like this.*[28]

Shortly thereafter Kindle, for whom Sassoon felt responsible because of his youth, was killed, spurring Sassoon initially to rage and a daring attack on the German sniper responsible, but leaving him to reflect sadly as he returned to headquarters, past the bodies of Kindle and the unknown young German, on the pointless loss of both young men.

Sassoon was back at division headquarters when the division was relieved from a long period at the front during the slaughter of the Somme. He waited at the crossroads to greet the returning troops, an anxious wait in pitch dark, lasting more than six hours.

> An hour before dawn the road was still an empty picture of moonlight. The distant gun-fire had crashed and rumbled all night, muffled and terrific with immense flashes, like waves of some tumult of water rolling along the horizon. Now there came an interval of silence in which I heard a horse neigh, shrill and scared and lonely. . . . The field guns came first with nodding men sitting stiffly on weary horses, followed by wagons and limbers and field-kitchens. After this rumble of wheels came the infantry, shambling, limping, straggling and out of step. If anyone spoke it was only a muttered word, and the mounted officers rode as if asleep. . . . I had seen something that night which overawed me. It was all in the day's work—an exhausted Division returning from the Somme Offensive—but for me it was as though I had watched an army of ghosts.[29]

Nothing could be more deflating than Sassoon's description of his journey to the field dressing station after he was shot through the chest some months later in the Battle of Arras. It evokes many earlier literary descriptions of hell and sets the scene for his journey "home" to a country in which he was no longer at home, as he had become an opponent of the government and the British military leadership.

> While we picked our way along the broken ground of Henin Hill I continued talkative, halting now and again to recover breath and take a last stare at the blighted slope where yesterday I had stumbled to and fro with my working party. The sky was now over cast and the landscape grey and derelict. The activities of the attack had subsided, and we seemed to be walking in a wasteland where dead men had been left out in the rain after being killed for no apparent purpose. Here and there figures

could be seen moving toward the Dressing Station, some of them carrying stretchers.[30]

In a London hotel converted to quarters for convalescent officers, Sassoon was astonished to discover that he and his fellow officers were required to listen to lectures on trench warfare delivered by a staff officer who had never seen battle. Among those ordered to attend were amputees without arms or legs and men blinded by shrapnel, men for whom service in the trenches was clearly impossible.

Sassoon, by then a much decorated infantry officer, decided to denounce the conduct of the war by the high command and to excoriate the government of the day for refusing to define a set of war objectives by which the general populace, and in particular the suffering soldiery, might be able to conclude that the country's war objectives had been reached. His memoir ends with a wryly comic chapter in which his superiors contrive a medical explanation for his defection from military duty and he is shipped away for treatment for "shell shock." There is no room left in this narrative for Burton's "great game" of Empire, there is only the tragicomic deflation of individual human desires in the face of the bureaucratic authority of a corrupt state.

Sassoon did not reach the point of denouncing all warfare and depicting all heroism as the result of the manipulation of individuals for dubious political purposes. But in the 1939–1945 War, which pitted the British and French empires against the German in Europe, and against Japan in the Pacific, the imperial hero ceased to exist for both the volunteer and the conscripted soldiery. One of the most striking statements of this change in consciousness appears in an Australian memoir about the kind of life a Stanley or a Burton seemed to relish, skirmishing in disguise in hostile territory. *Fear Drive My Feet* (1959), by Peter Ryan (b. 1923), chronicles the experience of an eighteen-year-old warrant officer in 1942–43. His story opens with the narrator sitting on a rock in the New Guinea jungle, just outside Wau, behind Lae and Salamaua, very recently occupied by the Japanese. He has been sent, without maps, compass or adequate food, to connect with a distant officer in uncharted country, an observer who radios news of Japanese troop movements to the headquarters of the

ramshackle army engaged in resisting the Japanese and protecting
New Guinea's main port, Port Moresby, from the invaders.

> It never occurred to me that I'd been given a pretty slim chance
> of survival by my superior, the district officer who had sent me
> on this errand. Nobody thought it very strange then, least of all
> myself, to send someone into that country without such basic
> necessities as food, maps, and compass. When you are eighteen
> the fact that quite stupid people can play chuck-ha'penny with
> your life doesn't seem too unjust. This is partly because the thrill
> of the adventure is more dangerously intoxicating than liquor,
> and you aren't too closely in touch with reality. You stride down
> the jungle trail full of confidence, a pioneer, a new David Liv-
> ingstone; you feel exactly like your favorite hero from Boy's
> Own Paper.[31]

After a year of collecting information in the jungle, Ryan returned to base in Port Moresby for medical treatment for his
malaria and jungle sores, but he quickly proposed that he return to
the jungle area he had just left. He knew that now it would be
crisscrossed by Japanese patrols, but he believed that a lone man
with a radio could live off the jungle, collect the information that
flowed from village to village and help alert the Australian defending forces to impending Japanese troop movements.

His choice was dictated in part by how he felt about the way of
life of an army headquarters. He could tolerate the danger of active
service, but he couldn't stomach what he saw as the shabby, profi-
teering ways of army life behind the front lines.

> In a fighting unit there was the comradeship of proved friends,
> the tradition of things endured together, which evoked a very
> definite generosity and loyalty. . . . By contrast, base areas, where
> living conditions were usually reasonably good, seemed to
> smoulder with petty and personal jealousies. . . . The black mar-
> ket in liquor, smuggled to New Guinea by service aircraft, made
> the civilian black market seem a gentlemanly affair. More often
> than not soldiers who were actually doing the fighting and tak-
> ing the risks seemed to be regarded with aversion, or at best tol-

erated as inescapable burdens who disordered the even routine of life.[32]

Ryan's life behind the Japanese lines involved extraordinary hardship, unrelieved risk taking and, eventually, an inexorable network of Japanese patrols closing in on their quarry. Moreover, the dearly won information he delivered was often misinterpreted or taken too lightly by headquarters in Port Moresby. Ordered back to base at last, he was within reach of safety when his party was attacked by Japanese in what had once been the safest village he could rest in en route home. He escaped by hiding in a muddy swamp, only his nostrils above the putrid slime.

> *For a few minutes all was quiet, but soon I heard the Japanese calling out to each other, and their feet sucking and squelching in the mud as they searched. I could not see, so I did not know exactly how close they were, but I could feel in my ears the pressure of their feet as they squeezed through the mud. It occurred to me that this was probably an occasion on which one might pray. . . . Then something stopped me. . . . I experienced a rather weary exhilaration that, terrified and abject, lying literally like a pig in the mud, I had not sufficiently abandoned personal integrity to pray for my skin to a god I didn't really believe in.*[33]

Having made good his escape, Ryan worked diligently to prepare maps and build airstrips for the Allied forces now, in 1943, swarming into New Guinea through Port Moresby. At a critical point in this phase of the Allied offensive, Ryan developed severe malaria, necessitating his evacuation to Port Moresby. As he walked down the jungle airstrip to the waiting plane, he passed a mortally wounded Japanese soldier being interrogated by Australian intelligence officers.

> *As I looked at his face, wasted with fever and suffering, I suddenly felt more akin to him than to the Australians who would not let him die in peace. His eyes, wonderfully large and soft, met mine. In that brief second I hoped he could read the message in my face.*[34]

His narrative ends with rejection of his own nationality and identification with all suffering soldiers in modern warfare. The personal mission of the romantic man of destiny is no part of his sense of self. In its place is an unpleasant awareness of having risked his life to little purpose. His disillusionment comes from reflecting on the dangerous life he has lived and recognizing

> *how useless your whole mission was, how futile and purposeless your death would have been, and, above all, when your sober but aching eye discerns that nobody whose business it might have been took the least trouble to see that you got at least a reasonable chance of living.*[35]

The experience of total war tended to eliminate the differences in self-presentation between women and men, so that both end up their stories of 1914–1918 or 1939–1945, or the Vietnam War, with the same bitter disillusionment, and the same moments of sympathy with the enemy. Vera Brittain (1893?–1970) begins *Testament of Youth* (1933), her memoir of her generation and its experience of the 1914–1918 War, with many feminine preoccupations. She recalls the way her pink ninon dress and rose-trimmed hat fitted in with the rose garden where she first spent time alone with the young man who was to become her fiancé, and shortly thereafter to die in the trenches in France.

As the slaughter of the war unfolded, and all her male friends were killed, one by one, her tone changes. One of her circle of friends was wounded in the Battle of Arras.

> *Victor had been wounded on April 9th at Arras, first in the arm—which he had disregarded—and then in the head, while leading his platoon to attack the inexorable redoubt known as "The Harp."*[36]

Victor, barely alive and blinded by his head wound, was awarded a Military Cross for bravery, something at which Brittain would have thrilled two years before. Now she reflects that her brother was also awarded this highest decoration for bravery, and that *"the attractions of being a hero were apt to lose their staying power when they were expected to compensate for severe physical damage.*"[37]

Brittain had left her sheltered and prosperous country life for service as a nurses' aide, so severe war wounds were now a reality to her, and her sense of heroism and the rewards of service significantly modified. We no longer hear about her dress, or its compatibility with the setting. She has ceased to be on view and has become an anguished actor and witness of the war's destruction.

Brittain saw the final stages of the war's destruction at No. 24 General Hospital in Étaples, where the last great assault of the German Army, reinforced with troops released from the Russian front, seemed likely to crush the Allied forces. Her hospital staff had no rest because there was no letup in the conflict.

> *Day after day, while civilian refugees fled panic-stricken into Étaples, . . . and the wounded, often unattended, came down in anything that would carry them—returning lorries, A.S.C. ambulances and even cattle-trucks—some fresh enemy conquest was first incredulously whispered and then published tentatively abroad. . . .*
>
> *Three weeks of such days and nights, lived without respite or off-duty time under the permanent fear of defeat and flight, reduced the staffs of the Étaples hospitals to the negative conviction that nothing mattered but the end of the strain. . . . To us with our blistered feet, our swollen hands, our wakeful, reddened eyes, victory and defeat began—as indeed they were afterwards to prove—to seem very much the same thing.*[38]

Brittain, like Sassoon, felt a permanent stranger at home in England. Her days and nights at field hospitals and the deaths of all the young men who had been her lovers and friends left her permanently grief stricken, distrustful of governments and repelled by the concerns for comfort and affluence once an accepted part of her comfortable world.

Nurses, even in 1914–1918, when they were often very close to the front, cared for the wounded after the first triage of the euphemistically named casualty clearing station. But in the conflict in Vietnam the patterns of warfare discreetly called anti-insurgency,

in which the front was everywhere, and the use of helicopters
to airlift soldiers immediately from combat to military hospitals
meant that nurses themselves treated the wounded minutes after
battle.

They ran the triage rooms, struggled to save blasted bodies,
slipped and slid around emergency rooms whose floors ran with
the blood of the wounded. It was they who told the victims of
minefields that their legs were gone, and they who fretted hope-
lessly about the eighteen- and nineteen-year-old soldiers left to die
alone because there was not time to be beside them.

These nurses' memories produced some of the most passion-
ately written accounts of the Vietnam experience, told in a form
similar to most male accounts of modern warfare. The story opens
with the establishment of the persona of the idealistic nurse—
patriotic, usually the daughter of a veteran of the 1939–1945 War.
First comes the shock of encountering the confusion and misman-
agement of mass armies, the poor quarters and makeshift hospitals
contrasted with the comfort and style of life of visiting military
brass.

Then comes the ambiguity of the struggle, questions about the
cause and the startled discovery of civilian victims of supposedly
friendly fire. After that there comes the discovery that people at
home don't want to hear about the experience, and that many are
actively hostile to Vietnam veterans. Finally comes the horror of
the inability to forget, the nightmares and the disruptive intrusions
of the past upon the present.

Winnie Smith's *American Daughter Gone to War* (1992) brings
every element of this shattering experience to life. Still an idealistic twenty-two-year-old, Smith began her tour of duty at the Third
Field Hospital, just a mile away from Saigon Airport. She had
come hoping to serve the Vietnamese people as well as American
troops, but that hope was complicated by the ambiguities of fighting an underground civilian army. Who was a friend and who an
enemy? Then came the horrified discovery of the weapons used by
American forces.

> [*Chopper*] *is a month-old Vietnamese baby on our ward whose
> tiny ribs gleam through the gaping wounds on his chest and
> back. . . . At first we didn't know what caused the wounds. Ul-*

cers? A tropical fungus or a microscopic worm? . . . It was the corpsman working with me tonight, a former field medic, who solved the riddle. Not ulcers but burns—napalm burns. . . . We were spared seeing Chopper on fire, but just imagining it makes me cringe. "How could the VC do this to their own people?" I ask, nodding to the corpsman to lift Chopper so I can rewrap the burns.

The corpsman squints. "The VC don't have napalm. We do."[39]

It was when Smith transferred from a medical ward to the intensive-care unit that her initiation intensified as each day brought its announcements of helicopters on their way with wounded, and she found herself making life and death decisions. Those around her bet she wouldn't last long—but she had found real work where she mattered.

This night marks the end of my first two weeks on the ward. All bets on how long I would last are now lost. My perception of hard work, of exhaustion, of tragedy is forever changed. They have become the facts of life, the standard by which we live and work, and I wouldn't have it any other way. I'm where I want to be—as close to a combat nurse as I can be, although I wear starched whites and work in an old French school.[40]

Still, she had difficult questions about the war. She and a friend wondered why the U.S. forces were bombing South Vietnamese villages to save them from the North Vietnamese forces. The stock answer was that the villages were infiltrated with Vietcong, but in fact it seemed that most southern villages supported the Vietcong. Then there were questions about the level of popular support for the South Vietnamese government, an inheritance from the French colonial regime, and it was that government, a French colonial inheritance, which favored the bombing of the villages. The questions that went along with the image of Chopper, the month-old napalm-burned baby, wouldn't go away.

Smith had trouble ever getting close to the men to whom she was attracted, because of the fear that within days she would be caring for their mutilated bodies. On the eve of her departure she dodged possible messages from one of the officers she'd been seeing at the time.

> *Whatever he has to say, I don't want to hear it. If Larry's dead, I don't want to know. If he's messed up for life, lying in some hospital bed without arms or legs, I don't want to see him. I want to remember him with a light in his eye and the catlike grace of a warrior.*[41]

Back home she suffered intensely from flashbacks, still unable to form enduring ties to other human beings she feared might be killed or mutilated. On Veterans Day 1984 she shared her sadness with a group of male veterans just her age.

> *We all survived the same way, by numbing ourselves to what was asked of us. They swallowed their fear in order to face the enemy. I buried compassion to face the wounded.*[42]

At the high point of imperialism in the late nineteenth and early twentieth centuries, the native peoples, the casualties of Empire, were carefully defined as other—those to whom the benefits of Empire and later progress were being brought. In the 1970s, at the end of the Vietnam War, there was still the impulse at home to define the casualties as other, although by now these were not native peoples but citizens of the United States. The participants knew beyond any hint of doubt who had paid the price of a global power struggle and that there was no coming "home" after such an experience. The knowledge was the same for women and for men, a form of equality no one had planned upon or expected to achieve.

CHAPTER FIVE

FEMINIST PLOTS

THE BOURGEOIS CULT of privacy concerning family and domestic life required women to be silent about their role in family
dramas. It also enjoined false modesty upon women, which silenced honest reporting. Because they had to preserve the family
secrets, nineteenth-century women wrote for themselves as di-
arists much more frequently than they wrote memoirs. The diary
allowed confidences no one else was supposed to hear. The mere
act of sitting down to write an autobiography broke the code of
female respectability, because doing so required a woman to believe that her direct experience, rather than her relationships with
others, was what gave meaning to her life.

So we should read feminist memoirs as conscious acts of rebellion. Writing and publishing one's life history was moving beyond secret rebellion to announce one's reasons for breaking the
gender code. But what was one to do with such rebellion? Could a
woman just reverse traditional gender categories, assume the persona of a female Odysseus and set about describing her heroic life
journey? Could even the most rebellious woman throw over the
dictates of cultural conditioning and convince herself, let alone
others, that she was her own heroine? Or did she have to contrive
some hybrid narrative—part quest for authenticity, part censored
report of an inner life, something closer to the medieval woman's
reflections on spiritual relationships to powerful enabling figures?

Nineteenth- and early-twentieth-century women had great difficulty making themselves subjects and objects of their own stories. But by the midtwentieth century we see new, more confident narrative styles emerging, although the self-denigrating female narrator seems a permanent part of our culture. In some women's stories the powerful *I* of the narrator is center stage—in others she is almost a voice speaking from another room, so skillfully is she concealed among the props of the drama. Memoirs full of abrupt transitions and shifting narrative styles are sure signs that their authors are struggling to overcome the cultural taboos that define these women as witnesses rather than actors in life's events. Whenever someone tells her story straight and in an authoritative voice, we know she has developed her own sense of agency and can sustain it despite nagging cultural doubts.

When Harriet Martineau (1802–1876) wrote her autobiography in 1857, she was fifty-five years old, stone deaf, and thought herself terminally ill. Certain death is a quick dissolver of cultural taboos, so Martineau, a woman who had become one of the leading educators of her society on social and economic matters, could throw away many concerns about privacy and modesty as she followed her daily practice of churning out a manuscript to meet a deadline. This time she wanted the world to know how she had become such a cultural phenomenon. For phenomenon she was. She had earned some ten thousand pounds from her writing by the time she was thirty-two, and her public constantly clamored for more of her essays and fiction. She was the popular interpreter of Adam Smith and Jeremy Bentham for the Victorian reading public, a force to be reckoned with until she laid down her pen in the mid-1860s.

Martineau writes with the authority of an accomplished public figure, clear-eyed about herself and her family. Nonetheless, it is her inner life which takes center stage in the opening chapters of her autobiography. Tormented by a punishing religious sensibility, she tells us her early life was dominated by the need to escape an overwhelming sense of sin. "I wanted to be at ease in conscience; and that could only be by growing good, whereas I hated and despised myself every day."[1]

Though she tells us she never spent a day without crying, Martineau's intellectual curiosity and precocious reading made this sixth of her family's eight children begin to find peace of mind. At the age of eight she discovered Milton's *Paradise Lost* in her father's library, and, she says, "my mental destiny was fixed for the next seven years." By the time she was sent, at the age of eleven, to a good day school, her reading had made her "a sort of walking concordance of Milton and Shakespeare." She found schooling "delectable" and soon began to put herself to sleep at night reciting Latin, as she had previously done by reciting large sections of *Paradise Lost*.[2]

As Martineau tells it, four converging forces combined to enable her to become the remarkable intellectual figure she was in adulthood. First, she began to grow deaf. The lost hearing she says, matter-of-factly, was "the best thing that ever happened to me." Deafness made it necessary for her to master her inner life, control her feelings and develop habits of personal discipline. Second, she was able to confront her mother and her sister Rachel over her mother's favoritism toward the younger girl. The successful challenge to maternal authority gave her a sense of power she had previously lacked.

Third, her courtship by and engagement to John Hugh Worthington ended in 1826 with her fiancé's death. So events beyond her control removed her from the life of the emotions she had been trained to experience. With hindsight she could see that she was unsuited for marriage, enjoyed solitude and was happiest alone. "I am probably the happiest single woman in England," she could write at fifty-five, after having proved that she could support herself and her family comfortably by her writing.

But the fourth and greatest influence on her life was her father's death, the loss of the family's modest means and their consequent loss of gentility. Martineau regarded these events, traditionally seen as disasters, as the happy circumstances that freed her from her false role as a gentlewoman obliged to be in society and gave her, she said, the "liberty to do my own work in my own way."[3]

Luckily, deafness precluded the usual resort of genteel women left penniless. Martineau could not become a governess or open a school. Instead, she had to settle down to write for a living. Little more than a year after the collapse of the family fortunes, Martineau had won enough literary prizes and secured enough contracts to publish her work to mark her freedom as an independent woman. Her first grand writing project, *Illustrations of Political Economy* (1832–1834), a popularization of Utilitarian ideas which involved formidable feats of learning, was a success within weeks of publication. She describes herself as "by thirty years of age, having ascertained my career, found occupation, and achieved independence."[4]

At the age of thirty-one she moved to a small London house where she could enjoy her literary career, a pleasure somewhat diminished when her mother and aunt arrived to live with her. She was unsentimental in describing the problem.

> *My mother, who loved power, and had always been in the habit of exercising it, was hurt at confidence being reposed in me; and distinction shown, and visits paid to me.*[5]

Visits were certainly paid to Martineau. Many chapters of her memoir are taken up with thumbnail sketches of the great and powerful who called upon her and the requests made to her by the government of the day, or the opposition, to support pieces of reform legislation. She was genuinely puzzled at the reliance others placed on her ability to affect public opinion by her writing. Yet by her forties she had come to enjoy being courted. "My life began with winter," she wrote, "burst suddenly into summer and is now ending with autumn,—mild and sunny." There were some clouds obscuring the sunshine, however. Having her mother and aunt in her house was a trial. They kept her in a constant state of emotional turmoil because they could not understand her work patterns or accept the social life she kept up as a single woman. The "constant troubling of the affections" they caused decreased Martineau's productivity and left her feeling drained.[6]

Like many a late-twentieth-century career woman, she felt impoverished about time. Pressure of work had made her obsess about the passage of even a few minutes. She felt compelled (almost like a female Benjamin Franklin) to use every second profitably. Yet the prospect of death allowed her to relax. "I find in the last stage of my life that I can play and be idle; and that I enjoy it."[7]

In fact she lived another nineteen years, although the abdominal tumor which caused her painful digestive problems and pressed upon her heart continued growing and caused her intense suffering in the last years of her life. Intellectually, Martineau lived into a vigorous old age, her life a combination of Franklin-like self-engineering and Rousseauistic emotional Sturm und Drang. We see in her a pre-Romantic woman freed to work by becoming déclassé, and inspired to question female roles by her dislike of what she saw as corrupt female authority. Her independent life in London and her role as interpreter of contemporary social and economic theories and trends were holdovers from the Enlightenment view of female rationality soon to be undermined by the popularity of Rousseau's focus on the romantic, intuitive female. Her motive for telling her life story came from popular adulation and her wish to set the record straight. An experienced writer, she told her story without shrinking from comment on family or sexuality, though she is in no sense a confessional autobiographer.

Elizabeth Cady Stanton (1815–1902), born in Upper New York State a mere thirteen years after Martineau, lived a young girlhood totally different from Martineau's. Her girlhood illustrates the relative openness of American society compared with provincial England in the early nineteenth century. The fourth child of a family of five daughters and one son, Stanton resented the fact that her father wished she'd been born a boy and fretted that her brother could leave home for study at Union College while she was not considered a candidate for higher education. Even though she was in her eighties when she wrote her memoirs, Stanton's anger at the injustice still shows.

When her brother died in Stanton's eleventh year, she pledged to herself that she would make up to her father for the loss of his only male offspring. Gradually it dawned on her that her efforts to excel in the study of Greek and mathematics at the local Johnstown academy, or become a fearless rider, were exploits that her father would have rejoiced in in a son, but they brought no similar joy when performed by a daughter.[8]

Even so, Stanton reports, she spent much of her spare time in her father's law office, listening to his conferences with clients and quizzing him afterward about the legal questions involved in the day's cases. In this way she learned the statutory basis for women's legal inferiority, and the common law tradition which limited women's rights. Moreover, Stanton tested her prowess in legal argument with the young students who were reading law under her father's guidance, picking up rhetorical powers which were later to make her an outstanding orator.

Although Stanton reveals obvious stresses within her family, and blames her mother for an overly strict, near "military" upbringing, she presents her youth in the opening chapters of *Eighty Years and More* (1898) as though she were part of an American pastoral idyll. So when she met Henry Stanton at her Abolitionist cousin's house during a summer vacation, the ensuing engagement, for which Stanton had sought no parental approval, seems like the natural pattern of an American romance. Certainly she makes neglecting to consult her parents about the match seem like simple absentmindedness, though so free and easy an action was hardly routine for young American women in the 1840s.

The idyllic romance is juxtaposed with the disapproval of Stanton's father (her mother is scarcely mentioned), a disapproval so profound that he painted a bleak picture of her future in this match. Her father's attitude, she says, "overweighted my conscience and turned the sweetest dream of my life into a tragedy." After hesitating, Stanton persisted and was married against her family's wishes. As she and her husband set sail for England and the first World Anti-Slavery Convention in 1844, she reports, "Fairly at sea, I closed another chapter of my life, and my thoughts turned to what lay in the near future."[9]

Stanton's narrative now shifts around like a wind chopping and changing directions before a storm. Her wedding journey to England, France, Scotland and Ireland seems to have been fraught with battles with her husband and his conservative antislavery colleagues over women's rights. No sooner had they arrived in London than the battle broke out between British Abolitionists and the Garrisonian wing of the American antislavery movement over the seating of women delegates at the London Anti-Slavery Convention. Tempers within the American delegation became heated over this issue, although the refusal to seat women gave Stanton the chance to become acquainted with women Abolitionists, such as the renowned Quaker preacher Lucretia Mott. Indeed, the great benefit of her meeting Mott was the pledge the two women took to organize a national convention on women's rights when they got back to the United States. Wherever Henry Stanton and his bride traveled, the issue of women's rights kept popping up, so their journeys were peppered with heated arguments.

Stanton grew weary of it and stayed in Dublin for a month while her husband and his party were touring Ireland.

> *Being tired of travelling and contending about women's sphere with Rev. John Scoble, an Englishman who escorted Mr. Birney and Mr. Stanton on their tour of the country, I decided to spend a month in Dublin.*[10]

On their return to the United States, Henry Stanton began the study of law in his wife's father's office, so she was back under parental tutelage, with her husband now somehow allied with her father.

Stanton's narrative now takes one of the abrupt turns which signal problems for the writer. Following the conventions which didn't allow women to mention the physical details of giving birth, she uses the birth of her first child as an occasion for an extended essay on motherhood, and the follies of contemporary medical practice concerning the care of infants. Her observations are true enough, but the placing of the essay disrupts the narrative and allows her to draw a discreet veil over her early married life. The following chapter gives a list of the reform circles in which the Stantons moved in Boston, where her husband began the practice of law, but makes no more than passing reference to the Stantons' personal life, then concludes abruptly with a sentence telling of Henry Stanton's poor health and the decision to move to Seneca Falls in central New York.

Once they had arrived in Seneca Falls, Stanton's narrative picks up again. She was a lonely, overworked, unloved mother of young children living on the edge of a small rural town. The sheer drudgery of daily life with young children, inadequate help and no sociability cast a woman for whom active intellectual life was a necessity into deep depression. When she had a chance to visit Lucretia Mott, who was staying nearby, she gave voice to long suppressed pains and discontents. "I poured out a torrent of my

long-accumulating discontent with such vehemence and indignation that I stirred myself, as well as the rest of the party, to do and
dare anything."[11]

On the inspiration of the moment, the group planned the famous Seneca Falls Convention and printed in the local newspaper
a call to the meeting, five days later. The drafting of the Declara-
tion of Sentiments, and a series of resolutions to be presented to
the meeting, occupied the intervening five days, with Stanton
adamant that Resolution 9, calling for the franchise for women, be
included. At this point the narrative really picks up speed. Stanton
tells us that she now had such a large range of interests, and had
gained such reputation and notoriety, that "my petty domestic an-
noyances gradually took a subordinate place."[12]

Very shortly after the Seneca Falls Convention, Stanton met
Susan B. Anthony, the woman who was to be her partner, guide
and friend for the rest of her life. Her description of the friendship
makes it clear that Anthony was more than a colleague and fellow
suffrage strategist.

> It has often been said . . . that she has been my good angel, al-
> ways pushing and goading me to work, and that but for her per-
> tinacity I should never have accomplished the little I have. On
> the other hand it has been said . . . that I forged the thunderbolts
> and she in the early days fired them. Perhaps all this is in a mea-
> sure true. With the cares of a large family, I might, in time, like
> too many women, have become wholly absorbed in narrow
> family selfishness, had not my friend been continually exploring
> new fields. . . .
>
> Thus, whenever I saw that stately Quaker girl coming
> across my lawn I knew that some happy convocation of the sons
> of Adam was to be set by the ears, by one of our appeals or
> resolutions.[13]

Stanton's memoir proceeds as a narrative of this relationship,
while Henry Stanton ceases to figure as a significant factor in her
account of her life. Stanton describes a partnership of the emotions and the heart as well as a political alliance with Anthony
which endured through many policy battles. When she tells us
that over thirty years she and Anthony never had a cross word, a

moment of jealousy or more than a fleeting difference of opinion, she romanticizes a relationship with many tensions over money, political allies, tactics and Stanton's tendency to get pregnant whenever her wandering husband paid a visit home. Nonetheless, "like husband and wife," she says revealingly, "each has the feeling that we must have no differences in public."[14] Whatever the conflicts, her relationship with Anthony was the sustaining bond of her adult years.

What made the two women's juices flow was the joy they took in politics, and their pleasure in strategic thinking.

> *Night after night, by an old fashioned fireplace, we plotted and planned the coming agitation; how, when and where each entering wedge could be driven by which women might be recognized and their rights secured.*[15]

Stanton makes it clear that it was the working partnership she valued and the commitment to shared goals which gave her a degree of psychic energy she had not possessed before she could count on seeing "that stately Quaker girl" crossing her lawn. Then, she had been sunk in "one of the most despairing periods of my life."[16] After the partnership with Anthony her psychic energy seemed inexhaustible, and the unhappiness of her marriage ceased to drag her moods down. Stanton's family had been correct in seeing that Henry Stanton's conservative temperament on all but the abolition issue would not blend well with her passionate radicalism. Judge Cady, Stanton's father, probably recognized that Henry Stanton was unlikely to be a success in either politics or the law, and that the relationship would bring his daughter only unhappiness and frustrated ambition. Certainly Stanton and her husband lived in separate residences for much of their married life, and she bore the financial burden of educating their five children. In her public life Stanton could blame the institution of marriage for her unhappiness, but inwardly she clung to an idealized picture of marriage, which kept coming out on family occasions.

Besides the partnership with Anthony, the high points in Stanton's narrative come from her progress as an orator and her growing confidence that she could win over a hostile audience by sheer force of rhetoric. One of the most telling incidents comes when

she recounts her inner triumph at swaying her father by reading him the speech on women's rights she was to deliver to the
state legislature in Albany early in 1854. Then aged thirty-nine,
Stanton describes herself as still needing to secure her father's
approval.

> *I described the widow in the first hours of her grief, subject to
> the intrusions of the coarse minions of the law, taking inventory
> of the household goods, of the old armchair in which her loved
> one had breathed his last, of the old clock in the corner that told
> the hour he passed away. I threw all the pathos I could into
> my voice and language at this point, and to my intense satisfac-
> tion, I saw tears filling my father's eyes. I cannot express the
> exultation I felt, thinking that now he could see, with my eyes,
> the injustice women suffered under the laws he understood so
> well.[17]*

None of Stanton's biographers has been able to verify this incident, which has the sardonic and wry-tongued Judge Cady in
tears. But even if apocryphal, the vignette captures Stanton's deepest motivation and tells us how she longed to be understood by the
men she loved.

Beside her pleasure in her powers of rhetoric, Stanton placed
the joys of campaigning, bearing the discomforts of travel and the
demands of a heavy schedule with undiminished enthusiasm for
the cause. Her first taste of sustained campaigning in frontier circumstances came with the unsuccessful 1867 campaign for suffrage in Kansas. The daily drives by carriage over the great open
prairies gave her a sense of the possibility of new beginnings in the
West, and she grew in her own estimation because her public
speaking was so effective and because she "could endure such
hardship and fatigue with a great degree of cheerfulness."[18]

Returned from the Kansas campaign to New York, where the
Stanton family now lived, Henry Stanton having exchanged law for
journalism, Stanton and Anthony made the choice which was to
widen their differences with New England suffrage leaders. They
accepted the sponsorship of George Francis Train, a financier of
dubious character and strong racist sentiments, for a new feminist

newspaper, *The Revolution*. Stanton writes that her two years as its editor were among "the happiest of my life." Her hard-hitting editorials, tackling the major issues of marriage, divorce and religious bias against women, gave full expression to her desire for relentless argumentation. She was happiest stirring up public contention, and mostly philosophical about the angry conservative response.

Shortly thereafter, having lost significant moderate feminist support, Stanton moved to Tenafly, New Jersey, and began to earn the income to support her five children as a lyceum speaker, spending eight months of the year on the road. Her narrative glides over the fact that this decision represented the necessity that she earn her living, and that it kept her distant from family life for three quarters of the year. The story is focused on the ease with which she bested her critics and the response she received to her rousing criticism of contemporary marriage in a much repeated lecture titled "Marriage and Maternity."

Her tone shifts dramatically when she describes the wedding of her daughter Margaret in the house the family occupied in Tenafly. The public critic of marriage as servitude shifts abruptly into high romantic mode. It was an October wedding in the garden, with the wedding party framed by the branches of old and majestic chestnut trees.

> *All nature seemed to do her utmost to heighten the beauty of the occasion. The verdure was brilliant with autumnal tints, the hazy noonday sun lent a peculiar softness to every shadow— even the birds and insects were hushed to silence.*[19]

Only weeks after her last lyceum lectures on the defects of the institution of marriage and the hazards of motherhood, Stanton slips into romantic pathetic fallacy in describing a family wedding. Did she seal off her family self from her public persona and simply live with the contradictions? Was she unaware of them? Was she faking the role of sentimental mother to please her daughter? Did she feel doubly compelled to stage the perfect wedding because she was a feminist critic of the institution of marriage? Probably all four factors were at work—certainly as the suffrage battle stretched out through the 1880s, she sometimes wondered whether she had

misplaced her energies, whether the vote was the strategic reform
to secure all other rights for women.

> *In asking for a voice in the government under which we live,*
> *have we been pursuing a shadow for fifty years? In seeking po-*
> *litical power, are we abdicating that social throne where they*
> *tell us our influence is unbounded? No, no! the right of suffrage*
> *is no shadow, but a substantial entity that the citizen can seize*
> *and hold for his own protection and his country's welfare. A di-*
> *rect power over one's own person and property, an individual*
> *opinion to be counted on all questions of public interest, are*
> *better than indirect influence, be that ever so far reaching.*[20]

The closing chapters of the story concern Stanton's children
and their marriages; work for the international suffrage movement; and the pleasure of working with Susan B. Anthony, Stanton's daughter Harriet Stanton Blatch and her son Theodore on
the multivolume history of the suffrage movement which was
Stanton and Anthony's last great collaboration.

The idealized vision of family life, maternity and child rearing
which this staunch critic held closest to her heart was revealed
only when describing family courtships, weddings and the arrival
of her grandchildren. The contradiction at the center of Stanton's
life, as we see it from the perspective of her eighties, was that she
still dreamed of the ideal Rousseauistic blending of two individuals
in marriage, even as her tough, legalistic intellect told her what was
wrong with the institution she herself had found such a prison.
The contradiction explains the silences about her own marriage in
her narrative, silences which make the story seem strangely two-
dimensional. Stanton was a captive of the American romantic temperament, even though she built her life as a reformer on rational
analysis of institutions.

Emmeline (Goulden) Pankhurst (1858–1928) began her memoir, *My Own Story* (1914), when she was in her midfifties. Her
book is a series of communiqués from a general in the field, and its
timing had more to do with her sense of a lull in the campaign for
women's rights, and the need to build North American financial
support for the cause, than with any point of acceptance or com-
pletion in Pankhurst's strife-filled life.[21]

The founder of the radical Women's Social and Political Union, the firebrand of the suffrage battle in Great Britain, Pankhurst has been criticized by many historians for the extreme methods of agitation adopted by the WSPU—methods thought to have delayed rather than advanced the suffrage cause. Recent feminist historians have questioned this assessment, arguing that, given the structure of power in British political life in the late nineteenth century, the militant activism adopted by the WSPU was indeed the program most likely to promote change. In the United Kingdom none of the three established parties—Tory, Liberal or Labor—stood to gain in electoral politics by endorsing the WSPU's program of votes for women property holders. Tories opposed such a change on philosophical grounds, while expediency required that they oppose all electoral change, since any change might undermine their disproportionate control of British legislation through the House of Lords. Liberals, meanwhile, were of necessity opposed to any change in voting qualifications which might enhance the influence of property in British politics, since the propertied classes supported the Tory Party. And the embryonic Labor Party, although sympathetic to women's rights, could not commit its full support to any program but universal manhood suffrage.[22]

Pankhurst's analysis was clear and very much in line with that of later historians—women could not win the vote by persuasion, since the forces opposed were too weighty and the government of the day controlled the legislative agenda. Temperamentally a radical activist, Pankhurst chose the method of agitation—nonviolent at first, but later increasingly violent—in order to change the popular perception of the issues surrounding votes for women and to compel attention to them.

Much has been made of Pankhurst's supposed neurosis, or martyr complex, expressed through her successful effort to recruit women activists to support the suffrage cause and to view it as a battle to the death, an all-out military campaign, with no room for negotiation or surrender. However, many Victorian women viewed the campaign for women's rights as a battle between the sexes, so that Pankhurst's rhetoric, which today sounds overheated, was well within the normal range of political discourse in her day. That discourse had been politicized by the struggle to repeal the Contagious Diseases Act, which undermined women's rights to privacy, treating them as sources of contagion against whom men had to be protected, and by the protracted struggle to secure the passage of legislation granting property rights to married women. Both struggles pitted women against men and were all the more bitter because they took place in a context in which an emerging male medical profession was defining all aspects of the female temperament as controlled by women's reproductive life.

The child of liberal Manchester reformers, Pankhurst grew up with the antislavery cause as the major family concern. It made her admire unyielding devotion to a moral cause and the courage necessary to defy public opinion. Moreover, she notes in *My Own Story*, her closest friend at her French boarding school was the daughter of a revered political exile, a man so dedicated to the Republican cause that he had endured but escaped from the dreaded Devil's Island penal settlement following a prison sentence for his part in the Paris Commune.

In this context Pankhurst was shaped by the mental categories of slavery and emancipation, revolution and reaction, seeing all issues in the formal political terms of her affluent Manchester background but unaware of the social and economic dynamics which undergirded the British political system.

Since she saw the Women's Social and Political Union as "a suffrage army in the field," her narrative reads like terse reports from the scene of battle. We hear nothing of her courtship and marriage beyond the flat statement that "my marriage with Dr. Pankhurst took place in 1879." Beyond saying that the marriage was "as nearly ideal as possible" and noting the births of her children, she shares nothing of its emotional and social context. There is no room on the page, nor was there in Pankhurst's life, for any story but that of her growth to leadership in the cause of votes for women.[23]

A close observer of British politics, about which she began learning as a child reading the newspapers to her father, Pankhurst saw that extensions of the suffrage to males were earned by threats and deeds of violence, such as the rioting and burning of hayricks, which secured the vote for agricultural workers. And, always alert to strategy and tactics, she saw the effectiveness with which Charles Parnell led the Irish Home Rule forces in the House of

Commons. By always voting against the government and contesting every seat where a member of the governing party might be unseated, Parnell eventually maneuvered the Liberal Party into a situation in which they could govern only with the support of the Home Rule forces, support which he made contingent on a government bill granting Irish Home Rule. Pankhurst aimed to do the same with the suffrage issue by showing that suffrage supporters could engineer the government's defeat at the polls.

These two lessons governed the strategy she laid out for the WSPU, which she formed in 1903, affiliated with no party, focused on the single issue of votes for women. Pankhurst rightly concluded that the annual meeting between members of the House of Commons friendly to suffrage and the women's suffrage organizations was a farce, since no private member's bill could secure the goal. The WSPU, then, was committed to securing the goal through political action, deeming earlier suffrage endeavors "outworn missionary methods," examples of persuasion when what was needed was political clout. What Pankhurst ignored or misunderstood was the extent of popular prejudice against women in politics, and the degree to which the government could exploit that prejudice against the suffragists.

The *I* in Pankhurst's narrative is permanently center stage, ever ready to seize the political moment. When the suffrage bill allowed to die in Parliament in 1870 was reintroduced by a Labor member in 1905, Pankhurst and a delegation from the WSPU were present along with other suffrage groups in the Strangers' Lobby. When they heard that discussion of the bill was being prevented by the tactic of talking out (protracted and frivolous discussion of the measure preceding it), Pankhurst recognized an occasion to capture their indignation for significant action.

> *Seeing their temper, I felt that the moment had come for a demonstration such as no old-fashioned suffragist had ever attempted. I called upon the two women to follow me outside for a meeting of protest against the government. . . . Instantly the police rushed into the crowd of women, pushing them about and ordering them to disperse. . . . This was the first militant act of the WSPU.*[24]

Pankhurst's strategy ran afoul of the strict codes regulating the Victorian gender system. Her incredulity and outrage still reverberate through her excited prose when she describes how the accepted male tactic of questioning candidates at political meetings on their government's policy if elected backfired because the questioner was a woman. Pankhurst's daughter Christabel and Annie Kenney, two young stalwarts of the WSPU, were detailed to question Sir Edward Grey, a likely cabinet member if the Liberal Party took office, at a political meeting in the Free Trade Hall in Manchester. Male questioners were courteously answered while the two young women's questions were ignored. As the meeting was breaking up, Kenney stood on her chair and shouted again above the rising hum of conversation: "Will the Liberal Government give votes to women?"

> *Then the audience became a mob. They howled, they shouted and roared, shaking their fists fiercely at the woman who dared to intrude her question into a man's meeting. Hands were lifted to drag her out of her chair, but Christabel threw one arm around her as she stood, and with the other arm warded off the mob, who struck and scratched her until her sleeve was red with blood. Still the girls held together and shouted over and over: "The question! The question! Answer the question."*[25]

Both women were dragged down the aisles by stewards and flung outside, where they instantly began to address the crowds until they were arrested for disturbing the peace. Tried and convicted, they each refused to pay the fine for their misdemeanor and served the prison sentence imposed by the judge.

Having made the cause news in Manchester, the WSPU transferred its attention to London, where a mass meeting was organized for the opening of Parliament in February 1906. When news reached the meeting that there was no mention of votes for women in the king's speech laying down the new government's policy, Pankhurst led a spontaneous demonstration through the cold rain and sleet to Parliament House, where the demonstrators were stopped by the police and initially refused admission, though later they were allowed in twenty at a time. The demonstration satisfied

Pankhurst's deepest longing—to be a leader who could command a following.

> *Those women had followed me to the House of Commons. They had defied the police. They were awake at last. They were pre-pared to do something women had never done before—fight for themselves.*[26]

Thereafter Pankhurst reports the way her troops moved slowly through the stages of heckling of male politicians, mass demon-strations and street corner speeches modeled on the Salvation Army method of recruiting, to the point when the WSPU was out-maneuvered by the Liberal government's decision to bring in a bill establishing universal manhood suffrage. This action removed the potential for Labor support for women suffrage and undercut the WSPU's goal of votes for women householders.

The fact that there was to be an extension of the franchise with no mention of women suffrage after some thirty years of campaigning led Pankhurst to escalate the campaign from speech and demonstrations to more antisocial behavior. Thereafter mem-bers of the WSPU broke windows, burned empty houses, dyna-mited postal boxes, poured acid on the tranquil greens of golf courses—executing their campaign with discipline, ingenuity and doubtless with the genuine delight at outwitting and puncturing male authority which was to become a common theme in later-twentieth-century feminist film and fiction.

The government retaliated by encouraging what modern soci-eties have come to call police riots. Suffrage demonstrations were broken up with violence accompanied by sexual assaults and cal-culated efforts to cause the maximum physical harm. Undaunted, Pankhurst led her troops to frustrate attempts to imprison them by adopting the hunger, thirst and sleep strike as a means of compel-ling jail authorities to release them rather than to appear to have caused their deaths in prison. Pankhurst has been seen as maso-chistic for adopting for herself and encouraging others to undergo such severe physical ordeals. Yet there is a well-documented ac-count of her resistance to the forced feeding by which prison au-thorities tried to control their prisoners. Hearing the struggles and cries of those in neighboring cells being forcibly fed, Pankhurst acted decisively.

> *In a few moments they had . . . flung open the door of my cell. On the threshold I saw the doctors, and back of them a large group of wardresses.*
>
> *"Mrs. Pankhurst," began the doctor. Instantly I caught up a heavy earthenware water jug from the table hard by, and with hands that now felt no weakness I swung the jug head high.*
>
> *"If any one of you dares so much as to take one step into this cell I shall defend myself," I cried. Nobody moved or spoke for a few seconds, and then the doctor confusedly muttered something about to-morrow morning doing as well, and they all retreated.*[27]

What she did relish was the bitterness of the struggle against opponents she saw as without redeeming qualities of any kind. She was almost alone as a feminist leader urging women to be physically fearless and psychologically undaunted by imprisonment and solitary confinement, qualities she showed herself on innumerable occasions, qualities later generations of feminists would come to value. She also enjoyed the international reputation her leadership of the WSPU gained her, particularly the celebrity status she experienced as a lecturer and fund-raiser for the cause in North America.

As a narrative *My Own Story* loses momentum in its closing chapter because Pankhurst immediately suspended all WSPU militant activity on the outbreak of the 1914–1918 War. The crisp, energetic prose is replaced by an idyllic picture of Pankhurst enjoying a respite in Christabel's Paris flat, the nerve center from which her daughter had directed the WSPU when its leadership in England was in jail. Pankhurst tells herself she owes the world "my own plain statement of the events which have led up to the women's revolution in England."[28] It is noteworthy that the scene with Christabel is one of the few moments in which Pankhurst acknowledges family feeling. Of her son and her two younger daughters there is no mention, though Sylvia and Christabel figure as political allies. *My Own Story,* in this respect, reads like a transposed narrative in the style of male self-reporting, in which family and private life are not deemed relevant to the "real" story of the narrator's public role.

Jane Addams (1860–1935), whom we met briefly in Chapter Three, was almost an exact contemporary of Pankhurst, knew the English militant suffragette and disapproved heartily of her tactics. We see the reason why on the opening pages of Addams's classic of American autobiography, *Twenty Years at Hull-House* (1910). Addams had an ego quite the match of Emmeline Pankhurst's, but she disguised it so brilliantly in her narrative that the reader is barely conscious of the *I* behind the gentle narrative voice.

Addams was the youngest child of Pennsylvania Quakers who had moved to establish a prosperous grain business in Rockford, on the Rock River in southern Illinois. Her father, John Huy Addams, was a political associate of Abraham Lincoln, and had been involved in the campaign which won Lincoln the presidency. In her memoir Addams recalls that the first time she saw her father in tears was the day he returned home to tell the family of Lincoln's assassination. Thereafter, she tells us, they kept the anniversary of Lincoln's death as a day of remembrance—work was set aside and the family reflected on the life of the Great Emancipator, sometimes reading aloud from his letters and speeches. Since her mother died when Addams was a toddler, her closeness to her father made her especially dutiful on such occasions, so that at the age of seven she began to wonder in her diary what she and her generation could do that would be like the work of the revered Lincoln.

Having taken on the mantle of Lincoln in childhood, Addams discovered as a college student that, as she wrote to a favorite sister, "I was born to run things."[29] Nor was her perception mistaken. She was a natural leader, a brilliant scholar, clearly a young woman of deep moral purpose.

Determined to escape the family's plans for a conventional marriage, Addams converted the customary college woman's "finishing" tour of Europe into a time of systematic study of social thought, puzzling over the moral issues of the emerging American industrial society, searching for the institution in need of reform that was a parallel to slavery. Moreover, on a quest for independence for a single, educated woman, she studied religious communities of women, looking for the insight which would help her create a new style of life for college-educated women of her generation.

After years of travel and study, she wrote home to the sister who was her lifetime confidante that she had come up with a "scheme" which would help unmarried, educated women move from being social anomalies to being socially useful in a totally respectable way. Attached to the letter was a detailed, step-by-step plan to inaugurate her new kind of women's community, which was to be located in an impoverished immigrant slum area of Chicago.

So the scheme was on paper, carefully sketched in considerable detail a year before Addams actually set foot in Chicago to carry it out. It involved renting a house in the poorest ward of the city, inviting other women college graduates to join her there, recruiting the support of the Philanthropy Committee of the Chicago Women's Club (on which the wives of many wealthy industrial leaders sat), gaining the support of pastors of the major churches in the city, the major newspapers and the city council. The women would then set out to be neighbors to the population of immigrant families crowded into tenements close by the meatpacking works and the other major industries. They *could* be neighbors because they all spoke European languages. So they could put their educations to good use, break down the social barriers rising between prosperous Americans and the new floods of European immigrants, and help in building a more democratic society. Moreover, the work would not be charity because it would be as much for the benefit of the college women as it would for the immigrants. If Pankhurst was the archetypal ideologue, Addams was the typical American pragmatist, ready to draw eclectically on many sources to come up with a solution to the problem of what young educated women should do besides being maiden aunts.

So, in the fall of 1889, began Hull-House, the model "settlement house" on which the volunteer settlement movement was built in major American cities, giving rise to many varieties of urban reform, from the profession of social work to a new understanding of the need for the involvement of government in unemployment relief. By the time she published *Twenty Years at Hull-House*, Addams had become a legendary figure. Never at the forefront of the suffrage movement, since she was more concerned to act immediately to tackle urban social ills, Addams was such an accepted American leader that Theodore Roosevelt chose her to place his name in nomination as the candidate for the presidency at the 1912 convention of his breakaway Progressive Party.

Like Pankhurst, Addams was deeply concerned with the health of women and children, the need for widows' pensions, the importance of regulating child labor, and she spent her days conferring, strategizing, delivering speeches to mobilize opinion on such subjects, writing endless letters in her nearly illegible hand- writing, instructing her network of reform-minded friends on how this or that campaign for legislation or volunteer action should be carried out. But when she wrote her autobiography, she gave it the name of a place rather than a person and deliberately disguised the way she had planned her life. There were probably few women in the America of Addams's generation with greater personal agency, but she presents the events of her life as if they had somehow just happened to her.

She makes no mention of the careful planning of Hull-House, writing, "It is hard to say when the idea of founding Hull-House first came into my mind, but if it did, it came when I was taken by a philanthropic worker to see the poor etc."[30] She makes the possi- bility that her actions were planned conditional. Then she makes the moment of decision one not of rational analysis but of sudden religious conversion, and the moment of conversion came not when she sought out an experience but when someone else took her there. In grammatical terms she is using the passive passive— the construction which removes the speaker the greatest possible linguistic distance from the action being described. Of course, when we check her diary for the time in question, it becomes clear that Addams initiated the visit to the East End of London.

Addams has chosen to narrate her life as though she were a ro- mantic heroine to whom things happen, and she has suppressed any reference to a desire for power to do good that she avowed openly in her most private correspondence. Her romantic self- presentation accounts in large measure for the immense popu- larity of *Twenty Years at Hull-House*, because the persona she gave herself fit smoothly with American romantic stereotypes. No one could react negatively to feminine power unsought but simply con- veyed by destiny or divine providence.

The very different tone of Addams's personal letters and the style in which she lived make clear that her narrative self-presentation was a deliberate choice. Addams never traveled without a companion who saw to the baggage, acted as a secretary and screened her visitors. Because of her habit of giving it away to anyone who seemed slightly in need, she never carried money, leaving it to the companion to manage the tips, pay the bills, buy the tickets and make the necessary banking arrangements. She was hardly a woman lacking in ego, and she was unusually self-aware.

Twenty Years at Hull-House was an attempt to recruit support for the settlement movement, for the social philosophy of cooperative democracy Addams espoused and for the finances of Hull-House, an institution whose needs could no longer be supported from Addams's personal resources. In so doing it helped solidify the stereotype of the romantic social reformer, the woman all feminine heart and intuition, without the faintest hint of executive talent. Addams's effortless prose, a model of Quaker simplicity, and her gift for the telling vignette which made her readers see and feel the dilemmas of immigrant life, made the book the classic it is, still read and studied in American schools and colleges ninety years after she wrote it. But her silence on her willpower, her motives and her management ability made it all the harder for later generations of American feminists to break the mold she had so artfully assisted in setting.

CHAPTER SIX

ASSERTIVE WOMEN

A LTHOUGH THERE WERE major changes of strategy and tactics within Anglo-American feminist movements in the early twentieth century, the self-reporting of twentieth-century feminists showed little change from its nineteenth-century origins.

Virginia Woolf (1882–1941) never set out to write a full-length autobiography, but she wrote a series of autobiographical essays posthumously published with the title *Moments of Being* (1976). They show us a narrator of genius tackling some of the key issues of feminism. Because of Woolf's distinctive, easy, almost conversational style, the reader hardly notices that she or he is being shown the injustice of patriarchal domination of women, the horrors of incest, the consequences of a social system which places no value on educating women and the astonishing liberation of moving from acceptance of a Victorian sentimental notion of marriage to Bloomsbury's easy and tolerant attitudes toward sexuality. But Woolf is instructing more powerfully than any polemicist through scene and character, and her genius at conveying inner experience.

There was a tradition of memoir writing for future generations in the Stephen family. Following the family pattern, Woolf began, at age twenty-five, a set of reminiscences written for Julian, the first child of her sister, Vanessa, though the piece is really a memoir of her childhood and adolescence. It is also an example of the exercises in writing Woolf set herself in her self-taught evolution as a writer. The family convention solved the problem of voice for the apprentice memoirist. She could represent herself as writing a "life" of her sister while setting out to convey a childhood and adolescence marked indelibly by the death of their mother Julia Stephen in 1895, when Vanessa was fifteen and Virginia twelve.

With the narrative skill that was to make her fiction a marking point in the evolution of the English novel, Woolf charts the shifting relationships in the complicated Stephen ménage. The second marriages of Leslie Stephen and Julia Duckworth brought together Julia's three children by her first husband, Leslie Stephen's mentally retarded daughter from his first marriage and the four Stephen children who were born to the second marriage, Vanessa, Thoby, Virginia and Adrian. The weight of the narrative develops from Woolf's tracing the effects on the Duckworth and Stephen children of their mother's early death and their father's selfish and often tyrannical grief. Stella Duckworth, Julia's eldest daughter, took on her mother's mantle of caregiver and was almost consumed emotionally by the demands of her grieving stepfather. Rescued just in time by an adoring husband, Stella lived only a few months after her marriage, so the family was once more plunged into grief, and Vanessa in her turn became the attentive female who had to cater to the whims of an irascible, neurotically parsimonious and self-indulgent paterfamilias.

> For us the tragedy was just beginning; as in the case of other wounds the pain was drugged at the moment, and made itself felt afterwards when we began to move. . . . Your grandfather showed himself strangely brisk, and so soon as we came to think, we fastened our eyes upon him, and found just cause for anger. . . . Now when he should be penitent he showed less grief than anyone. On the contrary none was more vigorous, and there were signs at once which woke us to a sort of frenzy, that he was quite prepared to take Vanessa for his next victim. When he was sad, he explained, she should be sad; when he was angry, as he was periodically when she asked him for a cheque, she should weep.[1]

Soon it became clear to the Stephen daughters that their mother's death had also placed them at the mercy of the incestuous passions of their older stepbrothers. Woolf describes the most persistent offender discreetly in her youthful essay, though she was later to write more factually about the details of his abuse. Her description is chilling nonetheless.

> *Nature we may suppose had supplied him [George Duckworth] with abundant animal vigor, but she had neglected to set an efficient brain in control of it. The result was that all the impressions which the good priggish boy took in at school and college remained with him when he was a man; they were not extended, but were liable to be expanded into enormous proportions by violent gusts of passion; and [he] proved more and more incapable of containing them. Thus, under the name of unselfishness he allowed himself to commit acts which a cleverer man would have called tyrannical; and, profoundly believing in the purity of his love, he behaved little better than a brute.*[2]

Shortly after her mother's death, Woolf became violently emotionally ill—hearing voices, physically violent, racked by physical pain, unable to sleep or rest. Neither of these subjects—her half brother's forced physical intimacy, and her bout of insanity—forms a part of the story of her coming of age, although its tone tells the reader that the household was no longer the safe place she described from childhood.

In "A Sketch of the Past," written when Woolf was approaching sixty, she speaks more directly. The conversational tone, with no raising of the narrative voice, only serves to emphasize her horror at the situation created by her mother's death.

She shows us a picture of herself as a six- or seven-year-old straining to catch her image in a hall mirror. She did this secretly, feeling that it would be shameful for anyone else to see her.

> *I must have been ashamed or afraid of my own body. Another memory, also of the hall, may help to explain this. There was a slab outside the dining room door for standing dishes upon. Once when I was very small, Gerald Duckworth lifted me onto this, and as I sat there he began to explore my body. I can remember the feel of his hand going under my clothes; going firmly and steadily lower and lower. I remember how I hoped that he would stop; how I stiffened and wriggled as his hand*

approached my private parts. But it did not stop. His hand ex-
plored my private parts too. I remember resenting, disliking it—
what is the word for so dumb and mixed a feeling?[3]

By describing the eminently respectable daily routine of the
Stephen household, in which Leslie Stephen was emotionally ex-
ploiting her sister and the Duckworth sons were sexually abusing
both Vanessa and Virginia, Woolf manages to convey the irony of
the male pretensions to virtue they represent, the way the young
women's lives had to be lived as entirely contingent on male pleasure and her inner rage that the world was so arranged that women
had to abandon serious work to make themselves socially attractive. She and her sister were isolated females in a world organized
for men.

In that world of many men coming and going, we formed our
private nucleus. There we were alone with father all day. Adrian
would come back from Westminster . . . then Gerald from
Dent's or Henrietta Street; then George from the Post Office or
the Treasury; and Thoby would be at Clifton or Cambridge.[4]

The two sisters struggled daily to find some status that would
enable them to exist in their own right, and not as adjuncts to the
men. Each Wednesday was an occasion for bullying from their father over the household bills. Woolf knew, but could not say, that
her father's brutal mistreatment was a compensation for not winning a place of honor among his male peers as a philosopher.
"Hence," she writes, "the horror and the terror of these violent displays of rage. These were sinister, blind, animal, savage."[5]

Nonetheless, the Stephen girls asserted their individuality by
study—Vanessa at the Royal Academy, Virginia, in her bedroom
with a tutor to teach her Greek. But for the women, though not
the men, Victorian society commanded that they be home and
dressed for company at 4:30 p.m. They had to be available to give
their father his tea and to entertain such visitors as called. In
language reminiscent of Harriet Martineau's, Woolf notes bitterly
how much time women had to commit to mindless sociability, a
diversion for their menfolk but an infuriating disruption for women
who wanted to devote their time to serious intellectual pursuits.

In "22 Hyde Park Gate," an essay written for the memoir club established by her Bloomsbury circle, where the rules required absolute honesty, Woolf expanded on the theme of fashionable society and its mindless demands on women, mixing tragicomedy with the darker story of her stepbrother's incestuous attachment to her.[6] George Duckworth, in reality intent on securing a rich and aristocratic wife, decided to present himself to the arbiters of London society as a dutiful brother, devoted to seeing that his two motherless sisters were introduced to society. This involved badgering the Stephen girls to acquire the necessary evening clothes, lecturing them on deportment and dragging them to dinners and balls at which they were ill at ease and bored. Eventually matters came to a crisis in which Vanessa refused to accompany George to any more society occasions. Then Virginia's Greek studies were interrupted by George's insistence that she accompany him for the rest of the season. Woolf piles up the details of a series of disastrous occasions, extracting every comic dimension from George's obsession with the aristocracy and her efforts to find conversational subjects from her study of the classics which would divert her ill-read and narrowly conventional hosts. The essay closes with Virginia home after another comically dreadful evening.

> *At last—at last—the evening was over. I went up to my room, took off my beautiful white satin dress. . . . Was it really possible that tomorrow I should open my Greek dictionary and go on spelling out the dialogues of Plato with Miss Case? . . . In a confused whirlpool of sensation I stood slipping off my petticoats, withdrew my long white gloves, and hung my white silk stockings over the back of a chair. . . . Ah, how pleasant it would be to fall asleep and forget them all!*
>
> *Sleep had almost come to me. The room was dark. The house silent. Then, creaking stealthily, the door opened; treading gingerly, someone entered. "Who?" I cried. "Don't be frightened," George whispered. "And don't turn on the light, oh beloved. Beloved—" and he flung himself on my bed, and took me in his arms.*[7]

There can be few less victimlike accounts of incest than this ironic treatment. What Woolf did not mention was that her stepbrother's abuse gave her such a fear of male sexuality that she would experience another breakdown followed by a long spell in a nursing home before being able to reach the self-confidence that enabled her to take up her writing career, and that when she did marry, she was to remain sexually frigid.

Pankhurst and Stanton looked to the vote to liberate women; Addams founded her alternative community to create a place in society for independent, educated women; and Woolf, as the world knows from its endless self-documentation, found her release in Bloomsbury, and in the company of men whose erotic interest was in other men. She went on to write some of the strongest feminist fiction and nonfiction to be produced in the twentieth century. She had no political movement or institution to preserve, so she could speak the truth as she saw it. She became an icon of the liberated female consciousness—sensitive, ironic, detached, capable of profound human insight because she embodied the androgynous blending of reason and intuition. And yet, we have to ask whether Bloomsbury was really the ideal moral world for the liberated woman, and whether in this respect Woolf's genius let her down.

Where might more rage and less ironic detachment have carried her? She would have been repelled by the compulsive style of victimhood so prevalent in the late twentieth century, and would have rightly insisted that human affairs are much more complex than the current confessional mode of autobiography suggests. In that heady moment in the early twentieth century, total sexual permissiveness seemed to promise Woolf and her generation a liberation we have yet to find. What if she *had* been able to think more deeply about male-female relationships? But of course to do so she would have had to acknowledge the rage, and question the laughter.

Mabel Dodge Luhan (1879–1962) deserves to be called the marathon memoirist of American modernism. Between 1933 and 1937 she published four volumes, entitled *Intimate Memories*, chronicling her life from her birth to a rich industrial and banking family in Buffalo through her four marriages, her expatriate years in Europe, her life in New York as a proponent and supporter of modernism and radical political causes, her retreat to New Mexico and her conviction that the rootedness of Pueblo Indian culture was the remedy for the maladies of the modern consciousness.[8] She was a feminist in the sense of claiming sexual freedom for women and rejecting bourgeois notions of propriety, though her analysis by Freud's American disciple A. A. Brill convinced her that women could not achieve the level of sublimation and cultural creativity of men. Brill's analysis encouraged her to reject father figures and to define mature relationships as ones in which there was no domination of one partner by the other, a goal Luhan understood but rarely reached. Brill also taught her the standard romantic notion that female sexuality could and should release the creative powers of male genius, a view that she put into practice in a variety of relationships with artists and writers, including her much publicized liaison with D. H. Lawrence.

Greatly influenced by Gertrude Stein, Luhan began her first volume of memoirs with a spare, muscular prose style and a taste for satirizing cultural pretensions. The later volumes are a catalog of famous people, places and events, often a stylistic jumble which lacks coherence until Luhan settles in Taos and meets Tony Luhan, the Pueblo Indian who became her fourth husband. In her encounter with the Pueblo Indians, Luhan experienced directly the fascination with primitive art and religion which was a key theme of modernism.

She began her memoir writing in her fifties, with a volume describing her childhood and adolescence. The structure of the narrative comes from Luhan's wish to present her life as a process through which she learned to become a strikingly powerful embodiment of the Feminine Principle (in Luhan's mind femininity could only be spoken of in capitals). Her capacity to enter into the experience of others she called "the only genius I have ever had." Genius was what she claimed, and it was the reason for her autobiography—for "these pages are given to recording its progress."[9] Not surprisingly the *I* of the narrator is prominent in Luhan's narrative. She had no wish to disguise her agency, and, being a follower of Nietzsche and Wagner, no care about being seen negatively in the bourgeois world she despised. The only child of ill-matched and unhappy parents, she claimed to have experienced no sign of love or affection from either of them. She described her formal education as dysfunctional, and ascribed her growth in aesthetic and psychological maturity to the lack of boundaries in her personality, prefiguring the views of many late-twentieth-century feminist psychologists.

> *This natural sympathy that I could feel was not voluntary exactly, any more than the changing colors of the chameleon who takes on the color he comes in contact with are voluntary. I was just naturally fluctuating and flowing all the time, wherever I found myself, in and out of the people I was with. I have always been myself and at the same time someone else; always able to be the other person, feel with him, think his thoughts, see from the angle in which he found himself.*[10]

She learned to see form and color from her school art teacher, Miss Rose Clark, "about the only artist in Buffalo." Though not able to convey the skills of hand and eye necessary to transfer vision to paper or canvas, Clark taught Luhan how to look at things.

> *I liked her. I enjoyed her special kind of vision. I liked to enter her world and see life through her eyes. She adored beauty. She saw nothing but beauty; all the rest she ignored. She lived completely through seeing and her eyes borrowed the energy of all her other senses, so that she not only saw with them but she heard with them, she tasted with them, she felt with them.*

Luhan concludes her description of the art teacher with a scene in the teacher's appropriately simple studio, where, despite her limited means, there was a collection of blue and white porcelain. As they drank tea together Luhan realized that "she was drinking *blue*, not tea."[11]

Such aesthetic concerns were set to one side by an early loveless but erotically satisfying marriage, ended, shortly after the birth of a son, by her husband's death in a shooting accident. Although Luhan makes a parade of frankness, she does not describe the scandal caused in Buffalo by her subsequent affair with her married gynecologist, though this was the event that prompted her family to ship her off to Europe, accompanied by a nanny and her infant son. *European Experience* (vol. 2, 1935) chronicles her further aesthetic education, a second loveless marriage and the gallery of rich and famous people who were guests in the Villa Curonia, the Tuscan country house she restored and decorated at great cost. Here again, the *I* in the narrative is meant to be center stage but is often displaced by the cameo portraits of the writers, artists and expatriate English society Luhan cultivated. The frequently comical result of her forays into European society, and her detailed descriptions of her sexual adventures, led to a splendid satire by Cornelia Otis Skinner, whose parody of *Movers and Shakers* (vol. 3, 1936), entitled *Dithers and Jitters: A Brief Digest of the Intimate Memoirs of Mabel Fudge Hulan*, published in 1938, might well have silenced the voice of a less self-involved writer.

Movers and Shakers has been the most frequently quoted of Luhan's volumes because it describes the salon she established in New York at the peak of its pre–1914–1918 cultural radicalism. Luhan made herself known to New York intellectual circles by the essay she published on Gertrude Stein in the March 1913 issue of *Arts and Decoration*. Stein, she wrote, was "doing with words, what Picasso is doing with paint. She is impelling language to induce new states of consciousness, and in doing so language becomes with her a creative art rather than a mirror of history."

Determinedly apolitical, Luhan mixed radicals, anarchists, writers, artists and businessmen at her soirees at her apartment at 23 Fifth Avenue. Always a willing sponsor of talent and promoter of discussion on social issues, she helped fund the pageant performed at Madison Square Garden presenting the cause of the Paterson, New Jersey, textile strikers. She came up with the idea at a meeting in which the IWW leader Big Bill Haywood was lamenting the lack of coverage of the strike in the New York press. But wherever ideas were involved she denied her own agency. "This idea was speaking through me," she writes. "I hadn't thought it consciously." Later she speaks of her suggestion as an inspiration which was totally involuntary.[12] She doesn't mention her financial support for the pageant, nor for the Armory Show which launched modernism for an American arts audience.

Her much publicized affair with the radical socialist John Reed was tempestuous from the start because Luhan couldn't comprehend the political world for which Reed lived. She wanted an affair which would put her at the center of his life. She had no interest in being a partner in larger political causes.

> *He brought F. in one night and they talked all the evening while*
> *I sat forgotten. They talked wildly—over the possibles: the possi-*
> *ble revolution, the possible New Art, the possible new relation*
> *between men and women. I felt defrauded and left out and also*
> *very mad to have such a common little thing spend an evening*
> *with me whether I wanted him or not.*[13]

Movers and Shakers describes in repetitive detail Luhan's energetic quest for the right soul mate and the right relation to nature
and culture. There were many volunteers to play the lover's role for
a rich and freethinking woman whose hospitality was famous, and
whose interest in sponsoring the work of promising artists was
widely known. Whenever an affair ended, she wrote that she felt

> *the old depressed nothingness, which was all I was without a*
> *man. Be he ever so unsuitable, a man was what gave me iden-*
> *tity, I thought.*[14]

Her efforts to cope with depression spanned the range of
popular theories on mental health, from Freudian analysis to
Christian Science healing, experiments with peyote, visits to medi-
ums, dance study with Isadora Duncan and, on the advice of her
psychiatrist, paid work as a columnist for the Hearst newspapers
and as an interior decorator. Nothing, however, soothed so restless
a temperament, forever alternating between simple life in beautiful country farmhouses and sudden forays back to elegant New
York apartments.

A third unsatisfactory marriage, to the Russian Jewish artist
Maurice Sterne, led Luhan west to Santa Fe, where Sterne had become fascinated with Indian art and with the grandeur of south-
western scenery. From Santa Fe Luhan moved to Taos, where she
met the Pueblo Indian Antonio Luhan, who became her fourth
husband and the partner with whom she finally learned to live in
harmony. This transformation is the theme of the fourth volume of
her memoirs, *Edge of Taos Desert* (1937).

Luhan had an instant reaction to the grandeur of the high
desert scenery. It filled her with the American urge to shed the
complexities of settled society and live a life in contact with na-

ture. It was nature on a scale she could settle for, and the isolation didn't make her lonely.

As she approached Taos for the first time, in the company of the problematic and brooding Sterne, she knew she was arriving at the right place.

> *The sun, with a great smile radiating from it, was just at the rim of the faraway horizon, level with our eyes where we paused to look about us. Its rays came to our faces straight and unobstructed across the gulf of the black Rio Grande Canyon over westward. The interminable desert beyond stretched between it and us like a soft darkened carpet. The little canyon we had come through had spewed us up out of its depths and we stood breathless in awe at the scene that stretched before us that was revealed only for the short time it takes a sun to sink below the edge of the earth when it is many miles distant.* [15]

In Taos, at fifty-eight, Luhan began to see her previous life as a series of neurotic fixations, her interest in sensation and aesthetic stimulation as a way of hiding from her deepest feelings, her compulsive quest for love a distraction from knowing herself. The life of the Pueblo Indians, a subject and conquered people, appeared to her freer, less driven by anxiety, more firmly located in nature than any of the worlds she had inhabited in her efforts to throw off the constraints of her Buffalo childhood.

Inevitably, for Luhan, there was a man associated with her newfound balance—but the relationship was not romantic. She understood that Antonio Luhan would never comprehend her old ideas of romantic love, and that she had to respect the boundaries set by his Indian culture. Never one to give up the idea of playing a grand role in society, Luhan still strove to be a patron of artists, and the interpreter of the wisdom of Indian culture to the rest of the world. But she felt *real* for the first time in her life, and able to set some boundaries to her own self. In time, because of her relationship with D. H. Lawrence, whom she invited to Taos hoping that the setting and his hostess would inspire great literary achievement, she became the prototype of the "earth mother" who would become the heroine of the conservative culture of America in the

1950s—deeply erotic, in touch with nature, profoundly maternal and the inspiration for male cultural achievement. The unbounded earth mother was to reappear in one strand of American feminist thought in the 1970s, though by then she was transformed as a central figure in lesbian feminist culture. Luhan would have been too deeply Freudian to comprehend this development, although the 1970s feminist rewriting of the Freudian story to place the mother at the center of female psychological development was the logical outcome of her efforts to exalt the feminine principle in art and culture.

Germaine Greer (b. 1939) masks her memoir of her childhood and growing up in Australia as a quest narrative about her search for her father, Reginald Greer. Written when Greer was about to enter her fifties, *Daddy, We Hardly Knew You* (1989) purports to be the story of Greer's successful effort to unmask her father's identity. But in the process she tells of her childhood and adolescence, her family history and her relationship to her fatherland. And, by describing her journey to Australia as a middle-aged woman intent on reconstructing her father's life, she is also able to conduct a conversation with the reader about her expatriate's sense of her native country, seen with adult eyes.

There can be no mistaking the meaning of her description of her father's first Australian home in Tasmania.

> *Launceston is potentially a pretty town, with the wide river moving sleepily to its serpentine estuary, kept snug by tight blue hills.*

But there is something awry with the scene.

> *Launceston has neither the poetry of workmen's houses marching in egalitarian rows up and down, nor the leafy elegance of a spa town, but an uncomfortable mixture of the two. Clots of suburbia have coagulated in the valley and grabbed the heights, with wasteland and pasture cropping out in between. . . . Flowers splurt out of gardens too small to hold them, spilling on to streets absurdly wide, up which cars occasionally wander, adrift on a sea of tarmac.*[16]

Nature is not the only thing awry in Tasmania. Greer found much to annoy her in the system of public record keeping and the people who administered it. She learned that she could not search the records of births, deaths and marriages herself but had to pay ten dollars to have a ten-year period searched for any name she cared to give. Since she was intent on tracking several generations of a family, her search turned out to be very costly. Worse, it was carried out by rude and inefficient people.

> *The Archives Office of Tasmania is a small and uncomfortable place. . . . A series of irritable young women and one languid young man vied with each other to avoid dealing with enquiries from the counter.* [17]

In the Veterans' Affairs Building in Melbourne, she read her father's file, always watched by a vigilant civil servant. In it she discovered shattering details of his wartime breakdown. She'd had a fantasy that she might be able to care for her father in his old age—but the truth was that she didn't make the time, and he died while she was far away. In any event, he had never liked her to touch him, and much of Greer's anger at males is uncovered as she reflects on the fantasy. "If I had but once held him unprotesting in my arms, I could have survived that dreadful afternoon unscathed." [18]

So the reader keeps meeting a younger Greer as she searches for her elusive father. As a teenager she had spent all her free time in the Public Library of Victoria. She'd liked the calm energy of libraries so much she'd wanted to be a librarian. Although Greer was never without a book, her mother told her she'd soon get bored with reading. It was foolish for her to aim at being a librarian. It would be far better for her to learn to play tennis and meet some nice boys at the tennis club. "These were the fifties," Greer writes, "and I was a freak waiting to be born." [19] The returned expatriate still fumed at Australian suburbia, and was still ready to explode with rage at her mother.

Greer's next stage in the quest was to explore her father's military experience in India, the country to which he was transferred after his breakdown on duty in Malta in 1944. On arrival in Delhi she enjoyed the sight of a sacred cow in the midst of the afternoon traffic and recalled her father's anger at and distrust of Indian ways. Cattle, he thought,

> *should be farmed and slaughtered for food in the Australian way. The Australian way seemed to him sensible, the right way. If I had told him that I have come to see cattle farming as a major abuse of the ecosphere, and of cattle, he would have been convinced that I was quite barmy.*[20]

After her fruitless inquiries at the hospital where her father was treated, Greer went to visit the shrine of the mother goddess at Sabtashrungi. The shrine figure is a painted rock, an image for the volcanic forces of nature that pushed it up through the plain. She knelt to pray there to atone for her impiety in wishing to dig up her father and his past. The reader knows she also went because the very action would have enraged him.

Back home in the English countryside, Greer found herself agitated by the questions running through her mind. Had her father loved her? Did he respect her? Why had he never spent time with her or confided in her? We can feel the emotional urgency of the need to know one's parents which comes from reaching midlife. When we are no longer the rising generation but the one headed for old age and silence, we begin to develop a new bond to our parents, and Greer makes no secret that this is what she was seeking. Her research in British military records yielded the first insights. Her father had been a code officer, probably one of the keepers of ULTRA, doing work so secret code officers were taught not to fraternize—theirs were lonely, high-pressure jobs.

The thought of her father's loneliness is the launching point for Greer's reflection on her own lonely youth. She remembers her graduation as a Ph.D. at Cambridge. She was alone amid all the celebrating families.

> *I had worked all my life for love, done my best to please everybody, kept on going till I reached the top, looked about and found I was alone. My parents were too ignorant even to appreciate what I had achieved. I thanked my lucky stars it was English poetry I had studied, so that I had the charms and*

*incantations to lay upon the wound in my soul. If I had chosen
to study dentistry or computer science I might never have won
through to happiness.*[21]

Greer eventually discovered that her father had faked his identity completely, had been raised by a foster family and didn't know
who his own parents were. Reg Greer was a habitual liar and had
been invalided out of the air force in 1944 because he developed
anorexia while serving on Malta. Such a discovery could evoke
compassion, but Greer focuses on the pattern of deception which
became part of her father's life, and on the unpleasant details of
his behavior in the office, where he had pressed unwanted atten-
tions on the secretaries. She also came to understand why he kept
aloof from his bright daughter—because her curious questions
about his past represented danger.

When Greer has solved the family mystery we meet her with
her mother, a seventyish woman in skintight clothes, still searching the beaches around her home for a possible husband. The two
women are locked in mutual hatred. Clearly Greer's hunger for renewed ties to family cannot be assuaged here. As Greer tried to tell
her about her husband, her mother's mind seemed to wander.

> *You know the best book I ever read about you? she said. It was*
> That Difficult Woman *by whatsisname.*
> *David Plante, Mother dear.*
> *It was the perfect wind-up. She must have known how I
> hated that book. . . . In her random onslaught Mother had hit
> home, slammed me in the solar plexus.*[22]

In this pungent narrative Greer has followed the family pattern
of playing with identities, at one moment playing with the point
of view of her father, at another adopting her own perspective.
Greer's own point of view is center stage whenever she can talk
about her family, her feelings, her sense of loss, but she does it always under the guise of talking about her father.

If we ask why one of the leading feminists in the British world
should feel obliged to adopt this narrative ploy, the answer probably lies in the extreme discontinuities of Greer's life. A full-scale
memoir, explaining how her ideas developed from her original

standard liberal egalitarian view of women's rights to her readiness
to worship fertility and to envy the lot of Hindu women, would require cutting very close to the bone, revealing all the major themes
of her inner life. It would be a riveting story but one Greer is not
ready to tell. The one continuity needing no explanation is her
feelings about Australia, her unhappy childhood and the fraud on
which the family identity was based. The fraud of the father and
the petty pretenses of Australian suburbia can be lumped together
easily. But they don't offer more profound analysis of what gave so
gifted a scholar her passion for exposing the pretenses of patriarchy.

While Greer was making her lonely journey through Cambridge, Gloria Steinem (b.1934, just five years older) was at Smith
College, having contended with a childhood and adolescence
which enforced premature maturity. Steinem's father had abandoned his wife and two young daughters, leaving them in the failed
summer camp in Northern Michigan which was his last effort to
support his family. Steinem's mother, Ruth, had given up a promising journalistic career to marry so that, as her world collapsed
around her, she sank into depression, dependence on barbiturates
and tranquilizers and eventually real mental instability. Her daughter came to see her as someone who needed to be cared for, worried about, someone whose brain was too addled to rely upon.
Someone who had always been like that.

When she wrote her first autobiographical piece, Steinem, like
Greer, adopted the role of narrator of a parent's story. Steinem was
an acknowledged leader at the peak of the 1970s wave of American feminism and a woman approaching fifty when she wrote
"Ruth's Song (Because She Could Not Sing It)" (1983). The story
is told in the first person, focusing on the point of view of her
mother, although the older Steinem also tells us a lot about her
teenage self in the process.

When Steinem got away to college and the sister who had
valiantly tried to be Ruth's caregiver couldn't manage and had to
get Ruth admitted to a psychiatric hospital, Steinem felt the relief
of the precocious caregiver. From her safe distance, she could
begin to acknowledge Ruth as her real mother and to wonder
about her past.

That wondering is recounted with sorrow and nostalgia by

a feminist who reports that her deepest emotions concern older people.

> *I've always been more touched by old people than by children.*
> *It's the talent and hopes locked up in a failing body that gets to*
> *me; a poignant contrast that reminds me of my mother, even*
> *when she was strong.*[23]

What she is also telling us is that feminist though she may be, she still defines herself as a caregiver, and it is in that capacity that she sees herself in the world. It was not until Steinem was approaching sixty that she could, as she tells it, "claim my own place."[24]

She had spent two decades traveling, speaking, raising money, arguing, strategizing, persuading, and eventually the woman who had made herself caregiver to all women in her mother's honor ran out of energy. Life had lost its zest and color, and she felt weighed down by the burdens of her responsibilities to others, and to the women's movement. "I'd been submerging myself," she writes, "not in the needs of a husband and children, but in the needs of others nonetheless."[25]

When she made that discovery, Steinem says, she set about understanding herself and her inner needs, a process she reported at length in *Revolution from Within*.[26] She learned that she needed to treat herself as well as she treated others. She points out that one defect of character of women socialized to care for others is to become overly dependent on being needed. A really liberated woman should not need others to be falling apart to be at her strongest.

> *For myself, learning this lesson was definitely a function of age. I*
> *wasn't ready to admit how deeply into my brain cells and viscera*
> *the social role had permeated while I was still within age range*
> *of its grasp.*[27]

So, at sixty, she found her authentic voice, after devoting much of her fifties to learning to listen to herself, and to acknowledge that ceasing being a caregiver would not result in annihilation of the self. She could now feel the authenticity she had always claimed for the female voice—moving beyond the claim to the actual experience. As a result, the prose of *Moving Beyond Words* is crisp and energetic. Steinem presents herself without the tone of sorrow and regret for the injustices of the past so powerfully present in her essay on her mother's life. She has learned to live in the present, savor the satisfactions it offers, and take life on her own terms.

It is instructive to observe these two strong feminists struggle with the problem of "voice," because their struggles show us that voice, the product of inner agency, doesn't automatically follow ideological rebellion. Strong feminists they may be, but it is in relationship to their fathers or mothers that they first begin to speak to the world about their lives.

CHAPTER SEVEN

DIFFERENT STORIES

HE PREVIOUS CHAPTERS describe how the conventions of
gender (as distinct from biological sex) have laid down the rules
about how a man or a woman should report his or her life.

What happens to self-narrative when sexuality is ambiguous
and a person feels at odds with governing gender codes? How do
women whose erotic interest is other women tell their stories?
How do men whose erotic focus is other men shape their narratives? Even more interesting, how do those rare individuals who
come to consciousness convinced that, whatever the biological
reality may be, they have the psyche and consciousness of the
other biological sex, tell their stories? And, at the risk of being
thought literal minded, do the narrative voice and manner of self-
presentation change when an individual elects surgical sex change
and assumes the outer physical identity he or she feels is congru-
ent with the inner self?

These are questions we can ask only about relatively recent
times, because the avowal of homosexuality has exposed individuals to legal hazards right up to the present in North America, and
surgical alteration of the sexual organs and treatment with the appropriate sex hormones became possible only decades ago.

To try to answer these questions is to embark on a journey
across such embattled cultural territory that the only certainty is
that the answers offered will give offense at almost every point on

the cultural compass. The first sin is undoubtedly the simple one of assigning categories. Why a special chapter on gay and lesbian memoirs when the authors could have been included in the analysis of feminism, imperialism, et cetera, et cetera? The answer for the purposes of this chapter is that the focus of attention is on the author's ambiguity about or conflict with the gender conventions which shape narrative.

The second cause of offense will undoubtedly be the selection of the works analyzed and the places of their authors within the politics of the gay or lesbian communities—for it will surely be argued that they are not "representative" of the myriad points of view to be found within highly complex and deeply divided subcultures. And this criticism will be correct, for in this chapter the works discussed are not chosen for "political representativeness" but as examples of the varieties of narrative strategies adopted, and for whatever light they can throw upon the development of self-narrative within these subcultures.

About the selection of narratives by persons who have undergone sex changes there can be little argument, for the category is established by physical reality, and the body of writing is so small that the problem of selection scarcely exists.

Plant Dreaming Deep (1968) by May Sarton (1912–1995) is one of the earliest memoirs reporting a lesbian life in post-Freudian America. The memoir takes its title from one of the author's poems, which develops the image of Ulysses, setting course for home after many voyages of adventure to take root in his native soil. The image is male, as is the one European ancestor whose portrait she hangs above a Flemish chest in the eighteenth-century farmhouse she has bought and restored in Nelson, New Hampshire. He stands for her European ancestry, Flemish and English, now to be blended harmoniously within her Nelson farmhouse.

Sarton makes her story the story of the house—its restoration, its pattern of life, her relationship to the village in which the house stands, her sensibility while living alone in it. She makes only passing references to her close bonds with another woman. The memoir is dedicated to "Judy who believed in the adventure from the start." Then, in describing her search for a place to put down roots after the death of her parents, Sarton refers to the ménage she inhabited in Cambridge.

If "home" can be anywhere, how is one to look for it, where is one to find it? For me there was no ancestral "connection" that might have drawn me here or there, no magnet that might have narrowed down the possible choices. I could settle anywhere within a wide perimeter of Cambridge, for I intended to keep what I would not part with, my life with Judy, my place in her house, and the friends of many years.[1]

There were in fact many "magnets" in Sarton's promiscuous life, of which one of the most enduring was her literary friend Judy Matlack, who taught at Simmons College and whose location did circumscribe where Sarton looked for her house. This tie modified her rootlessness considerably, but so did ongoing affairs with a number of other women. Her relationship with the Harvard anthropologist Cora DuBois was the most influential of these. But to tell the history of her tempestuous erotic life would have been to tell a different story from the New England idyll she wrote in *Plant Dreaming Deep.*

Sarton makes several more references to Judy, notably in a comic passage in which the two are in bed upstairs on the first night of Judy's visit to inspect the house. They are awakened by the sound of a moose bellowing, a frightening event for two urban people. But these passing remarks are the sum total of Sarton's direct self-identification as a woman bonded to another woman. They make clear what her emotional life was about but make no reference to the erotic nature of Sarton's relationships. Sarton makes explicit that her relationship to the house is a marriage of sorts—a quick guide to the reader that she looks for no other.

I have brought all that I am and all that I came from here, and it is the marriage of all this with an old American house which gives the life here its quality for me. It is a strange marriage and its like does not exist anywhere else on earth . . . and just that has been the adventure.[2]

So the memoir offers the reader a story about Sarton's New Hampshire house as a surrogate for her personal life. She makes the house and her rootedness there the reason she can accept that her life is past its meridian and moving inexorably toward old age.

*Growing old . . . why, in this civilization do we treat it as a di-
saster, valuing as we do the woman who "stays young"? Why stay
young when adventure lies in change and growth?*[3]

The New Hampshire farmhouse and Sarton's relationship to
the New England countryside around it are made to stand for Sarton's complete emotional life and her adjustment to her contemporaries, her profession as a writer and poet, her abandonment of
teaching—a change necessitated by narrow-minded reactions to
her 1965 avowal of her lesbianism. Sarton lost two jobs as a result
of this announcement, and of her openly lesbian pursuit of academic colleagues at Wellesley, but she left out of *Plant Dreaming
Deep* the reasons why a move to the country had become so essential. So the symbol of the house cannot quite carry the weight
Sarton's silence has loaded upon it. Sarton was a writer of such
talent that the reader almost forgets to ask why the move to solitude is necessary, but the question lingers. She was writing just a
few years before the new wave of feminism in the early 1970s,
which raised lesbianism as a political and cultural question that
had to be addressed in the struggle for women's rights within a
patriarchal political, legal and economic system. Sarton clearly
viewed her relationships with women as private matters to be managed as questions of style and taste rather than as personal dimensions of a major political and cultural issue.

Within six years, *Flying* (1974), by Kate Millett (b. 1934),
would treat the subject of lesbian relationships and their connection to the movement for women's rights with a degree of explicit
detail unimaginable for Sarton's generation. Millett's reputation as
a feminist was made by the publication in 1970 of her Ph.D. thesis
in English at Columbia. *Sexual Politics* argued persuasively that
there was a strongly antifemale bias in the canon of English literature, and that accepted English literary criticism either ignored or
endorsed this point of view.

Millett's book became one of the standard scholarly works
cited by feminist critics of official learned culture, and one of the
texts seized upon by feminists within universities who were arguing that women needed their own curriculum (eventually called
women's studies) to correct for the antifemale bias in Western
culture. This notoriety was something for which Millett was ill-

prepared, because her major interests were aesthetic—she worked as a sculptor and filmmaker alongside her academic career—and because she was coming to terms with her own bisexual erotic and emotional life and uncertain of whether her primary political commitments were to gay rights or women's rights.

She became a critical figure in the disputes between gay and straight women in the early seventies, disputes which temporarily split groups such as Betty Friedan's National Organization for Women, although NOW eventually became accepting of lesbian members and adopted parts of the lesbian feminist agenda. Shortly after Millett had appeared on the cover of *Time* as a symbolic leader of feminism, she was challenged at a meeting at Columbia to acknowledge her lesbianism. When she made her statement, she became a celebrity whose high profile exposed her to intense pressure from within the women's movement either to mute or to accentuate her message along lines favored by different wings of contemporary feminism. *Flying* is 546 pages of stream of consciousness, recording Millett's responses to her notoriety. Much of it, especially the passages describing her erotic life, both heterosexual and lesbian, could rival Joyce and Molly Bloom.

Because she was a doctrinaire supporter of the New Left ideology of honest communication, supposedly devoid of cultural "pretense," Millett conveys her life in a degree of detail which is mind-numbing for the reader who wants a fast-paced narrative. But cumulatively, if one can stay the course, she makes her life comprehensible, her narrative flowing seamlessly between inner monologue and description of outer events. From the opening pages the reader learns that Millett's sexuality is no longer a matter of private choice. She describes her "outing" at a panel on homosexuality organized jointly by the Columbia Gay Liberation and Women's Liberation organizations. She is married to a Japanese sculptor and introduces herself as a founding member of Columbia Women's Liberation and a bisexual. She thinks, mistakenly, that her sex life is no more the topic of the meeting than anyone else's.

> *Time stops: . . . my terrified mind stops remembering it, while Teresa Juarez's voice loud butches me from a floor mike center of the room, a bully for all the correct political reasons. Five*

hundred people looking at me. Are you a Lesbian? Everything pauses, faces look up in terrible silence. I hear them not breathe. That word in public, the word I've waited half a lifetime to hear. Finally I am accused. "Say it! Say you are a Lesbian." Yes I said. Yes. Because I know what she means. The line goes, inflexible as a fascist edict, that bisexuality is a cop-out. Yes I said yes I am a Lesbian. It was the last strength I had.[4]

The ensuing media furor, and the outcry against her avowal by conservative women's liberation leaders, triggered a nervous breakdown for Millett. She wonders aloud in *Flying* whether anyone has ever been driven mad by the media before, worries that her breakdown will return—that she'll never get back to writing and working in her studio. Most of all she dreads the loss of privacy after her appearance on a *Time* cover. The fear strikes when she has been uptown shopping and is hurrying home to prepare for a party.

Pop back into the subway. Get that chicken cooked. At last I can be unrecognizable again after Time *sold my image to strangers on airplanes. How satisfactory to be no one, a short rather plump subway rider, neutral, inoffensive. The perfect get-up to cancel a self. A subversive mind tucked under camouflage, plotting art or ideas. Then the guy next to me on the bench betrays me and leans over to ask if I'm Kate Millett. Crash into Astor Place goes the morning.*[5]

Millett buys the radical feminist view that individualism is a sin, and that what distinguishes women's culture is that women's groups function by consensus, without leaders. The feminist doctrine of the day taught that leadership was a male ego trip which women didn't want or need. Millett used some of her earnings from *Sexual Politics* to fund a women's filmmaking cooperative. They would make the ultimate underground film depicting the lesbian life.

I am the oldest of the company [she's in her midthirties]. I had just written some crazy book they had never heard of. And I had the bread. So I said we'll share it, make movies together, be a company. Then I wanted to go further, become a collective.

No very clear idea about what that meant, but it was the new
line against individualism.[6]

The style Millett has chosen for her narrative—a melange of
incomplete phrases and truncated sentences—reinforces an impression of a crowded, overly pressured life, in which political
causes and artistic projects are interwoven with a series of intense
and sometimes passionate relationships with women. These are
made more or less lurid in the light of pot and hashish in use in her
circle, and their steady drinking. The underlying theme of the story
is Millett's reliance on her husband, Fumio, and her desperate fear
that she can't be turned on sexually by most women. She can experience lust but not release. Release finally comes in a relationship
recounted in the closing section of the memoir, which describes
lovemaking in lyric detail. One of the concerns of feminist literary
critics like Millett was that women writers had never managed to
convey sexual experience as explicitly and powerfully as male writers, so Millett is clearly determined to correct the record—and she
succeeds.

She does so without apology, as concerned with documenting
every aspect of her way of life as any earlier revolutionary. She
is convinced that—although she is being ridiculed in the press,
regarded as totally suspect in academic circles, damned by her
New Left friends as an unregenerate capitalist because she's a successful writer—she represents a new way of life and a better, less
repressive morality. But, at the same time, she meets such unyielding hostility when she travels to speak at public gatherings, she
knows in her heart of hearts that, at least in her lifetime, the radical lesbian agenda will not be carried out. Her only shelter from
that depressing certainty is the intensity of her erotic life.

Will future historians say I blew it? Will they permit me my love
of Fire Island's summer, the ferry hitting the waves in the sun,
my glory over a long dress for a party in the Bowery studio in
winter. My passion for spirits like Celia Tyburn and Fumio.
Probably one should never feel such gaiety or despair.[7]

Millett is writing for future historians—trying to be honest.
But, even though she can admit that her women's filmmaking

cooperative became more exploitive than her rejecting family—
and that she can see herself getting entangled in an emotional relationship with a woman who resembles her mother—she still slips
into the romantic rhetoric she condemned in her academic writing
whenever she talks about love and social bonds. She does allow
the reader to see how much she enjoyed the money she made from
writing and speaking, but she structures her narrative in terms of
the romantic artist being consumed by her/his public. Seemingly
unaware that she is speaking like an unregenerate romantic, she
tries to record every aspect of her experience without apparent
apology while attempting to convince herself and the reader that
she's chronicling the beginning of a new world.

Millett leaves a few important elements out of what often
seems an overly detailed narrative. She certainly suffered the fate
of the individual whose life is taken over by events, chosen by the
media of the seventies both to represent the new wave of feminism
and then, after her avowal of her lesbianism, to discredit it. However, the original *Time* cover (August 26, 1970) was planned
through the efforts of Millett's publisher, Doubleday, and with her
concurrence. So she was a participant, although doubtless a naive
one, in what she came to call *Time*'s "appropriation" of her image.[8]

Almost a decade later, in *Zami, A New Spelling of My Name*
(1982), the poet Audre Lorde (1934–1992) tells the story of an
African-American lesbian life. In the early years of the gay rights
movement, it had been customary for African-Americans to define
homosexuality as a white problem, so the defiant tone of Lorde's
memoir is aimed at correcting the record. The third child of a
Grenadan couple who immigrated to New York in 1924, Lorde was
conscious in childhood that her mother, light skinned enough to
pass for white, was a powerful woman to whom others deferred.
The parents kept a united front before their children, never acknowledging the reality of white racism and how it affected them.

The parents kept such a tight rein on their daughters that
Lorde's adolescence was a time of warfare with them, culminating
in her decision to leave home as soon as she finished high school.
Proud and strong like her parents, she set about working her way
through Hunter College, only to be deflected by a failure in a summer school course. Looking for factory work to help her save
money so she could escape to Mexico, Lorde met up with Ginger,

the twenty-five-year-old African-American woman who introduced her to her first lesbian relationship.

Lorde says in the prologue to *Zami* that she had always wanted to be both man and woman,

> *to incorporate the strongest and richest parts of my mother and father within/into me—to share valleys and mountains upon my body the way the earth does in hills and peaks.*
>
> *I have felt the age-old triangle of mother father and child, with the "I" at its eternal core, elongate and flatten out into the elegantly strong triad of grandmother mother daughter.*[9]

She tells us that those feelings had been unexpressed, and her erotic drives literally not conscious, until her first encounter with Ginger.

> *I never questioned where my knowledge of her body and her need came from. Loving Ginger that night was like coming home to a joy I was meant for, and I only wondered, silently, how I had not always known it would be so.*[10]

Lorde's father's death broke up her pattern of life in Stamford, while her mother's overwhelming grief made Lorde even more determined to escape to Mexico. Settled in Cuernavaca and commuting to classes at the University of Mexico, she had time to notice and respond to nature, something her totally urban life had never allowed.

> *One morning I came down the hill toward the square at dawn to catch my ride to the District. The birds suddenly cut loose all around me in the unbelievable sweet warm air. I had never heard anything so beautiful and unexpected before. I felt shaken by waves of song. For the first time in my life, I had an insight into what poetry could be. I could use words to recreate that feeling, rather than create a dream, which was what so much of my writing had been before.*[11]

Returned to New York and Hunter College after a year in Mexico, Lorde experienced overwhelming loneliness. In the gay

Village world she was often the only black person. At Hunter she could take no one into her inner life.

> *Downtown in the gay bars I was a closet student and an invisible black. Uptown at Hunter I was a closet dyke and general intruder. Maybe four people knew I wrote poetry, and I usually made it pretty easy for them to forget.*[12]

Most of the time, she tells us, she was content with her loneliness. She was different in ways no one else was, and she had to give up trying to become close or to really share experience with others. But by the mere fact of giving up she was forced to confront her loneliness, and to grow strong enough to manage it.

The management brings her to what many straight readers see as the repetitive part of most gay memoirs, female or male—the accounts of one initially passionate affair after another, all subsiding in mutual disillusionment, pain and renewed loneliness, although, of course, the relationship in the closing chapter is always described as the ultimate romantic blending of erotic and emotional union. But Lorde doesn't see it that way.

> *Every woman I have ever loved has left her print upon me. Where I loved some invaluable piece of myself apart from me— so different that I had to stretch and grow in order to recognize her. And in that growing we came to separation, that place where work begins.*[13]

The work was the work of re-creating herself through looking back to the traditions of her Grenada and Carriacou women ancestors, and learning to take pride in her blackness and her own physical being. Zami, the name she takes at the end of her narrative, stands for the new self, still able to draw on the strength of legendary Grenadan women.

Judging by her creative ability, she was not deceiving herself. She published five volumes of widely acclaimed verse before she was fifty, and became a much loved professor of English at Hunter College. There she became mentor to generations of writers and an important bridging figure between black and white feminists.

What *Zami* doesn't tell the reader is that Lorde married at age twenty-eight, bore two sons and divorced in 1970. Nor does *Zami* make any reference to the other major crisis in Lorde's life—the discovery in 1978 that she had breast cancer. She described her subsequent mastectomy and cancer treatment in *The Cancer Journals* (1980) but left the experience out of *Zami*, which she wanted to be a mythic celebration of female eroticism. By editing out maternity and the signs of her own mortality, Lorde could build a triumphalist narrative about the strength derived from women's love for women. Many male narratives neglect to mention the birth of children and illness, lest it undermine the image of male power the author seeks to project. In appropriating a narrative of strength and agency, Lorde is adopting a style previously used by males, though her narrative voice is profoundly different. Obviously, she doesn't want to claim that she has also incorporated elements of male lovers into her persona—so her marriage can be an incidental aspect of her life, not relevant to her purpose of creating a mythic story of female power.

We see in these narratives many elements of earlier autobiographical traditions—the romantic quest for the ideal partner capable of complete erotic and emotional response to the beloved; the self-created individual who can draw on no models from family or history; the search for the ultimate earth mother, who represents primal Oedipal power, and of course the effort to rewrite a female life claiming many attributes of the Greek hero's agency. We can also see the suppression of discordant elements in the life story to fit a political purpose. What is new is the primary focus on erotic experiences and the assumption that erotic experience—as opposed to maternal experience for women or the fulfillments of public life for men—is *the* experience which gives meaning to life.

In *Cures: A Gay Man's Odyssey* (1991), Martin Duberman (b. 1930) tells the male side of the story, with the narrative talent of a skilled historian and the successful playwright's grasp of scene and dramatic pacing. His is the story of worldly success juxtaposed with the inner turmoil of a gay life in an academic world which discriminated openly against overt homosexuality. Its main theme is the author's struggle for a cure for his erotic drives, which a punishing society, and in particular its medical and psychiatric professions, defined as sickness. Duberman attended Yale as an undergraduate, earned his Ph.D. in American history at Harvard and soon after graduation took a position in Princeton's History Department. It was a dream academic career, marked by early esteem and success.

> *The more secure I became in my status as an intellectual, the less gloom I felt about being—as the psychiatric establishment then insisted—a disabled human being. I did implicitly accept the culture's verdict that I was defective, but could now somewhat circumscribe the indictment; I no longer felt wholly unworthy—merely crippled in my affective life.[14]*

The problem was that Duberman was entrenching himself more deeply in a scholarly life at a time when the very scholarship which was his ideal defined him as deviant. He would take a break from work to cruise the gay scene, only to return to his study and his diary to write out a new set of good resolutions.

> *My revulsion is working overtime. All sorts of resolutions. Eager for work—never going to waste time bar-hopping again, etc. No satisfaction there anyway. All set for return to analysis; must have a wife and family, only possible things that matter.[15]*

Dr. Weinraupt at Harvard was followed by Dr. Igen at Yale and Karl in New York. Each new effort at analysis was launched with vows to control Duberman's sex life and followed by a sudden reversion to the world of bathhouses and Fire Island summers. Work was Duberman's real way of keeping on an even keel. He published successful books, won scholarly prizes, began to write plays which earned critical acclaim, was granted tenure at Princeton and began to experiment with making his classes more profound interchanges between faculty member and students. But the "cure" eluded his most strenuous efforts. Whenever his libido heated up, he took on more scholarly projects to make sure he had no time for what his therapist of the moment saw as backsliding.

Historian that he is, Duberman carefully chronicles the intellectual roots of psychiatry's attitudes to homosexuality. In its American version, Duberman argues, the psychiatric profession of his day could not deal with Freud's often repeated assertion that all human beings have the capacity to be bisexual. So the best defense was hostility to homosexuality—the behavior that suggested Freud was right. Added to this was the fact that in the United States the profession was predominantly Jewish. Most psychiatrists were persuaded of the mistaken view that the Nazi hierarchy had been riddled with homosexuality—the sources of the hostile diagnosis he encountered seemed clear.

No matter how compulsively busy, Duberman felt locked in "deep feelings of aridity and hopelessness." Married friends would congratulate him on his creativity and envy his solitary way of life.

> *I had to check the impulse to shout, "Moron!—if I didn't have to expend so much energy fighting loneliness, I'd be writing* twice *as much as now!"*[16]

After writing a successful play, *In White America* (1964), Duberman moved to New York, aware suddenly that the world was larger than his academic colleagues and that he had talents which were valued outside academe. Meanwhile the movement for gay rights was about to surface in the Greenwich Village he made his home. But his connection with it was delayed by his last foray into therapy, with Karl, who practiced group therapy along with seeing patients weekly in private sessions.

Duberman's talent for character and dialogue takes the reader into the group sessions, which are comically horrible. His story detailing Karl's efforts to detach Duberman from family and friends, and to insert himself into Duberman's successful academic career, is told at such length that the reader marvels that such an intelligent man can be blind to such blatant manipulation. Duberman is brilliant as a historian analyzing the failures of academic and political leadership, but in 1968 he still blindly trusted the authority of his psychiatrist. An active opponent of the Vietnam War, and an early and vocal supporter of the civil rights movement, he is shown in his writing to be well schooled in unmasking corrupt authority in every case but his own search for a psychiatric cure for his homosexuality.

When a violent police raid on the Stonewall Inn sparked the first Gay Liberation demonstrations in New York, Duberman was a silent sympathizer but not a participant, still working hard in Karl's grotesque group therapy sessions and still making trips to hustler bars, the tougher part of New York's gay scene, about which he completed the play *Payments* in 1970. Clearly his creative writing was taking him in quite the opposite direction from his therapy.

The emerging change led him in 1970 to leave Princeton and accept a distinguished professorship at City University just when Karl suddenly abandoned his New York practice. The narrative now picks up speed as Duberman completes a striking new history of Black Mountain College, the culturally radical educational community in North Carolina which had been a pioneer of the avant-garde from the 1930s to the late 1950s. Duberman had discovered that its most valued leader in the 1940s had been forced to resign because of an arrest for homosexual activity—and the incident stayed in his mind as a possible frame for his own "coming out." His decision to announce his homosexuality in the preface to *Black Mountain* (1972) ends the narrative's dramatic tension. Thereafter Duberman finds his intellectual home in the fledgling Gay Academic Union, and, because he's connecting with a group of intellectual equals, he eventually meets there a partner with whom some mutuality is possible.

Duberman's story underlines one of the main themes in Gloria Steinem's later writing—that the process of freeing oneself from harmful gender stereotypes is lifelong, and that the ability to question authority in one area of one's life doesn't necessarily extend to others. His gay life begins with deeply romantic stereotypes about what a love relationship should be, although it quickly moves toward a penchant for cash relationships with good-looking young hustlers. His intellect and historian's training make him ask more provocative questions about sexuality than most gay writers, who are every bit as influenced by romantic myths as the heterosexual world. His training in standing back to look at the events being analyzed allows him a degree of humor usually lacking in stories of difference, or indeed any romantic narrative.

When he goes to Princeton he is recovering from a bout of genital herpes, which in the early sixties was treated with "warm soaks." This gives him a wonderful sentence to launch his account of his Princeton years.

So here I was at Princeton, fall of 1962, cock in a sling, psyche on hold, students bright and stuffy, colleagues pleasant and stuffier, career booming.[17]

Such high spirits reassure the reader that Duberman's narrative will see him to his goal of finding the ways to bring his sexuality and intellectual life into some working harmony—though the predominant tone is one of outrage and barely suppressed anger. Indeed *Cures* draws its tension from the question of whether or not the author will succumb to "expert" authority. There is a distinct falling off in narrative drive in the last chapters, as though this man needed his enemy to sustain the trajectory of his life.

As James Merrill (1926–1995), a near contemporary of Duberman, tells us, "My good fortune was to stay in one place while the closet simply disintegrated."[18] His is not the story of the search for a cure in the sense of seeking to be "healed" from a sexual orientation seen as an illness. He had the security of wealth, a powerful father, a clinging mother and adoring academic mentors who helped him find the gay life he so obviously sought. His urge to "make a name for myself" isn't the literal one of having to make his way in a profession but the self-imposed one of wanting to achieve in some way that will rival his father, Charles E. Merrill, the founder of the legendary brokerage firm Merrill Lynch.

The title he chose, *A Different Person* (1993), is a play on words which operates at many levels. Merrill wanted to be a person of substance yet had to battle patterns inherited from both parents—his father's compulsive womanizing and his mother's dependent clinging. He knew from his college years at Amherst that he wanted to be a poet, but at age twenty-four, when his memoir opens, he hadn't the discipline, the control of language or the experience to know how to write or what to write about. Always cared for by servants, he found it terrifying to be alone—something of a barrier to the writer's life.

When he set out for Europe in 1950, he was on a quest to become "a different person," but he knew he meant to *stay* different in the sense of being gay. His mother was intent on making him heterosexual and respectable, a young man to be introduced to proper society. But Merrill had observed "society" on weekends at the family houses in Southampton and Palm Beach and wanted no part of it. His father, on learning about his son's faculty lover at Amherst, first thought of hiring someone to murder the lover but eventually subsided into undemanding tolerance for his son's way of life. Merrill, speaking in his sixty-six-year-old voice, thinks his parents' efforts to change him tolerably moderate.

> As expressions of mid-twentieth-century prejudice go, these of my mother and father seem harmless enough. Hundreds of thousands of parents—not just mine—must have spent the forties and fifties urging secrecy and repression upon their queer sons.[19]

That wasn't the way he had felt as a younger man, when his mother opened his mail, took advice from lawyers and doctors about how to change him, insisted he see a psychiatrist and used the opportunity of his absence in Europe to destroy all the letters he had kept from friends. That action left him bereft, with no evidence that anyone but his interfering mother had ever loved him. She was afraid he'd be blackmailed, not realizing that someone who lived openly as a homosexual wasn't really a target for any such extortion.

Rome, where Merrill settled, and Greece, which he visited regularly, were more tolerant settings for an openly gay life than Duberman's Ivy League world, so when Merrill decided upon psychiatric therapy in Rome, his homosexuality was accepted, and the purpose of the exercise was to free him from the destructive behavior patterns learned from his parents. He saw that he clung as tenaciously to loveless relationships as his mother did to his father, and that the way he had related to lovers had many elements of his father's compulsive inconstancy. Dr. Detre, Merrill's Roman psychiatrist, is a benign figure whose insights heal.

Merrill felt shyness and overwhelming anxiety at the world of ideas. Theology, Greek philosophy, critical theory put him in a tailspin. He saw the world and his experience in it entirely in terms of imagery. So his memoir is a series of vignettes. The text, set in two different typefaces, contains the images of his growing up in his early twenties followed by his sixty-six-year-old perspective on those events.

In 1950 in Rome he stayed in a suite at the Excelsior Hotel with his father and an entourage of attendants. One of the events of the stay was a visit to the Pope. Nineteen fifty was an anno santo, so many pilgrims made their way to Rome for the blessing that came with an audience with the pontiff. Merrill was amused to see that on the morning of the audience his father was resplendent in a double-breasted white silk suit, color-coordinated with the Pope.

> *Many other pilgrims lined the audience chamber, but my father and the waxen, white-robed ascetic now making his way towards him—two men who had "reached the top" in their respective fields of godliness and finance—eclipsed the rest of us, in my view, like some long-awaited conjunction of Jupiter and Pluto.*[20]

The sixty-six-year-old Merrill recalls that at that time his father had just six more years to live. And his memories of him are surprisingly gentle.

> *To this day he remains an almost perversely mild and undemanding presence in my thoughts, triggering none of the imaginary confrontations I have with my mother. His company, by those last years, was an end in itself. As part of his entourage, I no longer questioned how to improve the hour. I didn't care if I ever wrote another poem; I lay back, contented, in the very arms of Time. It was a contentment I strove again and again to recapture.*[21]

There were some hazards to living in the cocoon of his father's wealth, and his father's determination to make the external world respond to his wishes. Merrill remembers thinking as a young man that life with so many retainers bent on securing one's pleasure could become bland, even boring. Many decades later, on an autumn visit to Rome, he surprises himself by ordering a crème caramel for dessert. Convinced he doesn't care for dessert, he finds himself nonetheless delightedly scraping his plate clean. As the afternoon lengthens into dusk, the crème caramel persists in his consciousness.

The light deepens. Now only do I recall that crème caramel was my father's great weakness, often ordered twice a day, during our long-ago time in Italy. Today, moreover, this very Sunday, October 19, is his birthday. He would be one hundred and one years old.[22]

Returned from Rome, analysis completed, literally a different person, Merrill settled in Stonington, Connecticut, with David Jackson, a fellow writer and companion for some fifteen years. Just when he had found his voice and pace as a writer, when his persistent loneliness has been dispelled by life with a stable partner—he encountered a final emotional crisis.

Just then, when life had never been more fulfilling, the genetic angel, as in a parody of the Annunciation, struck. What was this—nearly thirty and not yet a father! If through childlessness I'd been spitefully putting my parents in their place, parenthood would put me in theirs; how else to make peace between the generations? But I had better act quickly lest I be too old to enjoy my children.[23]

The comic search for a suitable mother was resolved by Merrill's analyst, Dr. Detre, now conveniently moved from Rome to New York. The emotional upheaval was about settling down—Merrill should take up teaching again and produce intellectual children. As the narrative moves toward its beautifully mannered conclusion, Merrill has arrived at a sense that what he wants is to be *used* by life, not to live always in an environment tastefully decorated but almost devoid of human feeling and passion.

His travels now took him more to Constantinople, where if his tastes dictated he could enjoy the male brothels but where he could also see the wonders of Byzantine culture. There he collected the talisman he most cherished, a street vendor's trinket, symbolizing all his apprehensions of the numinous,

a kind of pendant or pennant, chevron-shaped and fringed, entirely made of tiny glass beads: blue-green, white, orange, lemon yellow, pink. At the center, on a perch of beads, a beaded bird swayed; above it, beads spelled out MAŞALLAH (*Glory be! Praise the Lord!*). . . . *It's the perfect souvenir: a translation into the demotic of Yeats's golden bird on its eternal bough.* . . . *The talisman* (*readily unstrung, but who isn't*) *keeps up appearances, reminding us how notions such as Joy or the Imagination—the Holy Ghost Itself, if it comes to that—out of some recurrent urge to be embodied, make for a Halloween trunk full of feathers and wings.*[24]

Merrill always believed that a good poem should be difficult to decode, the power of its central imagery slowly growing upon the diligent reader. His pleasure in image and disguise and his cheerful manipulation of time sequence and points of view make him a postmodern memoirist, less certain of the direction of life's journey, more conscious of all the autobiographical texts which have preceded him. He was not interested in what he called postmodern "letting our lives hang out in vivid, one size fits all attitudes." "Who needs the full story of any life?" he asks, aware that the live person always remains different from the text.

The narrative drive in this story is Merrill's quest to become an authentic adult, to grow in emotional balance and creative power, to see deeper into things. Although he produced a 17,000-line magnum opus, *The Changing Light at Sandover* (1982), it scarcely figures in his memoir. It was not his work but his network of relationships Merrill felt important to describe—seeing meaning in life in a manner essentialist feminists were to claim as exclusively female. The "success" Merrill describes in the concluding chapters is emotional balance and the capacity for mature bonds to others. The critical acclaim, prizes, honors, place in the American literary pantheon didn't warrant a mention.

If James Merrill was seeking to figuratively become a different person, James/Jan Morris (b. 1926), the British journalist, sought to literally become one through surgical sex change at the age of forty-five. *Conundrum*, the memoir published under the name Jan Morris in 1974, tells the story of Morris's life as a male convinced he is a female entombed in a male body, and his decision in 1972 to have the surgery which would make him "as female as science could contemplate."

I interpreted my journey from the start as a quest, sacramental
or visionary, and in retrospect it has assumed for me a quality of
epic, its purposes unyielding, its conclusion inevitable.[25]

Morris was three or four years old when he realized that he
should have been a girl. The youngest of three brothers raised by a
widowed mother, his childhood sunny and his disposition cheerful, Morris kept his conviction to himself until his midtwenties.
At first his belief that his sex was mistaken was a blur at the
back of consciousness, accompanied by perpetual puzzlement. But
as he entered young adulthood, he knew that the central theme
of his life would be the ambition to "escape from maleness into
womanhood."

What he meant by womanhood was stereotypically female for
the late 1930s and '40s, and assumed that there was some unchanging essence of maleness or femaleness. His conundrum came
from having the wrong essence for his male substance.

My own notion of the female principle was one of gentleness as
against force, forgiveness rather than punishment, give more
than take, helping more than leading.[26]

Likewise he had conventional and somewhat condescending
notions about the female body. These come out when he describes
a journalistic assignment to cover the British expedition that
climbed Mount Everest in 1953. He liked and admired his excel-
lent male physique and felt it well tested when he accompanied
the expedition as a very keen and competitive twenty-seven-year-
old. He was lean and fit, and responded with intense pleasure
to physical challenges. So he was able to beat the other members
of the press down to the first staging camp, where it was possible to cable the awaiting London *Times* to announce the expedition's success. This kind of physical capacity he saw as exclusively
masculine.

Though I resented my body, I did not dislike it. I rather admired
it, as it happened. . . . It was lean and sinewy, never ran to fat,
and worked like a machine of quality, responding exuberantly
to the touch of the throttle or a long haul home. Women, I

*think, never have quite this feeling about their bodies, and I
shall never have it again. It is a male prerogative, and con-
tributes no doubt to male arrogance.*[27]

So in his beliefs about the physical and emotional aspects of
being female, Morris was what later feminists were to describe as
an essentialist. To him there was some essence of being female
that he experienced despite his male genitalia. His language about
that essence is vague of necessity, but the general drift is not too
different from later ideas about the essential female psyche, shaped
by life lodged in a network of relationships.

*To me gender is not physical at all, but is altogether insubstan-
tial. It is soul, perhaps, it is talent, it is taste, it is environment,
it is how one feels, it is light and shade, it is inner music, it is a
spring in one's step, or an exchange of glances, it is more truly
life and love than any combination of genitals, ovaries and hormones. It is the essentialness of oneself, the psyche, the fragment
of unity. Male and female are sex, masculine and feminine are
gender, and though the conceptions obviously overlap, they are
far from synonymous.*[28]

With these feelings, Morris's role in the British army, to which
he fled at seventeen to gain some relief from the barbarities of
boarding school life, was that of an observer more than an involved
participant. He felt himself on an adventure to watch a quintessentially male organization at work. He enjoyed the domesticity
of the officers' mess in a good regiment, liked to hear the catty gos-
sip of his fellow officers and enjoyed the clublike atmosphere of
a group of men sure of their class background and place in life.
But out of his feeling of definitely not belonging, he built his later
career as a journalist and travel writer.

After the war he began the long and frustrating search for
understanding of his transsexual identity from Harley Street psychiatrists and sexologists. These took him to be a transvestite, a
repressed homosexual, a freak. But Morris himself was beginning
to understand sex as a continuum, a biological marker which fluc-
tuates in expression in terms of the psychological concept of gender, which he took to be unvarying. So he began to wonder, if he

could not change his understanding of himself as a gendered being, whether it might be best to alter the physical marker of sex, and thus bring psyche and body into harmony.

At this point he met a woman with whom he established such rapport that they agreed to marry and establish a family, even though Morris made his predicament and ultimate goal quite clear. The marriage was for procreation and for companionship, but good sex was certainly not its raison d'être. As the family grew, Morris enjoyed considerable success as a journalist, working for the Arab News Bureau, *The Times* of London and the *Manchester Guardian*. As his reputation grew he found his male professional identity suffocating. He kept constantly on the move to evade the complications of settling in as a male in the community where his wife and family lived, but eventually the pretense became too much and he decided to undergo endocrine therapy, followed by surgical sex change.

During the hormone therapy he felt himself slowly changing—less taking on female form than shedding male characteristics.

> *The first result was not exactly a feminization of the body, but a stripping away of the rough hide in which a male person is clad. I do not mean merely the body hair, nor even the leatheriness of the skin, nor all the hard protrusion of muscle; all these indeed vanished over the next few years, but there went with them something less tangible too, which I now know to be specifically masculine—a kind of unseen layer of accumulated resilience, which provides a shield for the male of the species, but at the same time deadens the sensations of the body.*[29]

Eventually the change was sufficient for him to pass as a woman, a role he took up living in Oxford, apart from his family. There he began to wear skirts, female adornments such as jewelry, a feminine hairstyle; he started to adopt the internalized male gaze to assess whether he/she looked attractive. He also noticed that people began to patronize him, and treat him as a person whose opinions were of no consequence.

Next came surgery in 1972, performed in Casablanca, from which recovery was relatively easy. Returned to England, Morris experienced euphoria and woke each morning to an overwhelming sense of liberation. This happiness didn't evaporate, even when Jan Morris began to experience all the ways women are defined as inferior within the social system. People used a different tone of voice speaking to Jan Morris, their body language expressed less respect, at a restaurant the waiters ignored Jan Morris and assumed that the other party was the one to whom attention must be paid. The social cues began to take effect.

> *The more I was treated as a woman the more woman I became. . . . If I was assumed to be incompetent at reversing cars, or opening bottles, oddly incompetent I found myself becoming. If a case was thought too heavy for me, inexplicably I found it so myself.*[30]

She still had to resign from the all-male Travellers' Club, to dispose of the now useless dinner jacket and to inform *Who's Who* of a change of sex. Jan Morris found herself becoming psychologically less forceful, more likely to dissolve into tears; she paid much more attention to her appearance, and felt that stepping out on the street was an exposure to the "world's appraisal" that required careful preparation. But these changes were of no consequence compared with the release from the obligation to play the male role.

Morris's second volume of memoirs, *Pleasures of a Tangled Life* (1989), published in the author's sixties, is devoted to the sources of happiness in a long life. She wanted to provide a counter-narrative to the story of painful sexual ambiguity which was the central theme of *Conundrum*. The resulting set of autobiographical essays is pleasantly lighthearted and focuses more on recollections of Morris's male years than on her recent past. The one sign of her new identity comes in the startling assertion "All the best sex . . . aspires to the condition of incest."[31] She now lives as a woman with a female partner, and clearly doesn't want to think of the relationship as lesbian. Here we see Morris continuing to view her life from the standpoint of the sexual stereotypes she grew up with in the 1930s and '40s, despite her late-twentieth-century transsexual experience. The second volume describes no progression in understanding of what it means to be a woman, because for Morris there was no room for such a question. To be female was to have the right bodily components and experience the fixed core of femininity which is the eternal female. On this belief Morris had built his/her life, and her account of its later stages is flat and contains no tension or struggle for development. She tells her story differently because she sees nothing to tell beyond the surface narrative of dress and deportment.

It's probably necessary to believe in essential maleness or femaleness to have a transsexual experience. What is striking about such beliefs is that they concern a perception of maleness or femaleness which is unchanging—so that having arrived at the longed for identity, the narrator doesn't expect growth, new perspectives on life, all the usual accompaniments of adult life stages. Gay men's and lesbians' life stories, by contrast, contain all the usual reports of change and growth, though what is reported as important experience tends to blur gender categories—so that the patterns associated with men's or women's self-reporting don't fit. James Merrill's account of a network of relationships and Audre Lorde's celebration of female strength are stories in which one could change the pronouns and have no clues from the text as to whether the speaker was male or female. So the genre of gay and lesbian autobiography calls attention to human androgyny, while transsexual life stories can't be told in any but essentialist terms.

CHAPTER EIGHT

GRIM TALES

IF POSTMODERNISM MEANS anything, it's the abandonment of the idea everyone over fifty was raised on—of linear development or universal progress. Three converging trends in twentieth-century history account for the change. Belsen, Dachau, Hiroshima and a chilling array of regimes sustained by terror and torture make it hard to believe in progress. Then there's the problem that has heated up the culture wars in contemporary America. Europe's vanishing empires no longer support the belief that there is one central point in the world from which it may be viewed. We now see the arrival of Columbus at least from the point of view of Europeans *and* the American Indians who watched those first rowboats arrive. Once we thought pure adventure inspired Columbus and his crew. Now we know that Europe was running out of wood and needed new sources of fuel. That matter of fuel prompts attention to the third important trend. Even though we may rejoice in increased life expectancy, and confidently anticipate the arrival of a less polluting energy system based on hydrogen, there is no question that modern industrial technology and its accompanying standards of consumption for Western Europeans have resulted in major environmental disasters—so that the Victorian faith in science and its applications has now been replaced by ambiguity. Because we're not sure about progress, can't be certain all scientific discoveries will be beneficent and see our twentieth-century European patterns of consumption as dangerous for the environment, we've lost our sense that there is one history of progress, and we feel dubious about narratives told from a single, all-encompassing point of view. How did the arrival of Columbus seem to the Caribs he and his crew first encountered? Would those East Coast Indian tribes have thought twice about providing the corn and turkeys for the first Thanksgiving had they known the despoliation that was to come?

Along with the changed sense of time and the abandonment of a central cultural point of view has come a new kind of narrative authority for the young, for ethnic subcultures, for those of different sexual persuasions, for the handicapped, for victims of abuse—in short for anyone whose questions about life fall outside the central narrative of worldly success, or of moral and spiritual growth, or of power and its exercise—once the main themes for autobiographical writing.

In this closing decade of the twentieth century, there has been an outpouring of autobiographical writing by women and men in their thirties and early forties, focused not on reflections about the unfolding of a long life but on urgent questions of identity and relationships to parents. So what Rousseau introduced as a first chapter in his *Confessions* now occupies an entire volume. Of course, since postmodern literary theory has deconstructed narrative by pointing out the ways narrative structure expresses power relationships within a society, a postmodern author can begin and end a story wherever she or he likes. And since one does not have to have climbed to some position of power or eminence in society to claim that one's experience is exemplary, anyone's story is as good as the telling.

Kathryn Harrison (b. 1961) and Mary Gordon (b. 1949) both explore their relationships to manipulative and obsessive fathers and the ambiguities of a Jewish heritage in families of mixed religion. Harrison's story, *The Kiss* (1997), is not, strictly speaking, a memoir, because she makes no attempt to place her incestuous relationship with her father in any social, political or cultural context. The narrative reads like one of the more chilling of Grimms' fairy tales, opening and closing with a magical kiss—a corrupting one from her father and a healing one of farewell to her dead grandfather. Harrison is a writer of extraordinary talent; she manages to sustain the mood of obsession, or semimagical, dream-

like attraction, throughout the story. Some such device is necessary, because the reader can't help wondering why such a bright,
energetic college student takes so long to see through her seedy,
manipulative, unattractive father.

Harrison's story is constructed in Freudian terms, so that we
are shown her rivalry with her mother and her drive to displace her
in her father's affections. That drive was fueled by her rage that her
mother left her in the care of her grandparents at age six, moving to
an address her daughter wasn't allowed to know. Harrison never
gives a full description of her father—she describes his eyes, his
wandering hands, and his penis. Faceless and only partially embodied, he becomes for the reader just the force of his lust, a presence rather than a fully delineated human being. His eyes were
spellbinding—always, when he visited, turned on his twenty-year-
old daughter.

> *I don't know it yet, not consciously, but I feel it: my father, hold-*
> *ing himself so still and staring at me, has somehow begun to see*
> *me into being. His look gives me to myself, his gaze reflects the*
> *light my mother's willfully shut eyes denied. Looking at him*
> *looking at me, I cannot help but fall painfully, precipitously*
> *in love.[1]*

When her father left, he kissed his daughter good-bye, a kiss of
sexual passion rather than parental affection. Harrison makes this
erotic moment the point at which she lost all agency and became a
passive victim of their mutual desire.

> *In years to come, I'll think of the kiss as a kind of transforming*
> *sting, like that of a scorpion: a narcotic that spreads from my*
> *mouth to my brain. The kiss is the point at which I begin,*
> *slowly, inexorably to fall asleep, to surrender volition, to become*
> *paralyzed. It's the drug my father administers in order that he*
> *might consume me. That I might desire to be consumed.[2]*

The story which follows is of Harrison's long, passionate affair
with her father. She departs from the tradition of incest narrative by making clear that, however exploitive the relationship
may have been on her father's part, it was also, at least initially,

passionate on hers. By presenting herself as utterly under the control of her erotic drives, Harrison is portraying herself as the ultimate romantic female. She could have stepped from the pages of Rousseau's *Émile*—the perfect mirror to her father's needs and desires, someone totally lacking in the capacity to act on her own behalf. Indeed, if we take the sexual dynamics of this story to heart, 150 years of feminism might never have existed for the twenty-year-old Harrison.

Harrison's capacity to act on her own behalf was given to her by her grandparents' love, by her grandfather's and her mother's deaths, and by the care of a skillful psychiatrist. Only with these could she become a moral being, exercise choice, dismiss her father from her life, begin the graduate study her intellect clearly craved and proceed with her life. In traditional fairy-tale style, the spell she'd been under was broken by a good kiss—the one she gave her dead grandfather when she sat with his body for an hour in the hospital morgue.

> *I expect to be frightened by this corpse I have fought to see, but how can I be? The face and hands above the sheet are so familiar that what I feel is a rush of affection. . . . I kneel beside him, I lay my head on his chest as I used to when I was small. I touch his eyebrows and his cheek, the white stubble of his beard. . . .*
>
> *Though I've courted and teased death, played irresponsibly with my life, I never believed in my own mortality until I sat beside my grandfather's cold body, touched and smelled and embraced it. All along it was my unbelief that made this recklessness possible. The hour I spend with my grandfather, kneeling by the long drawer, changes my life. The kiss I place on his unyielding cheek begins to wake me, just as my father's in the airport put me to sleep. I am transformed from a person who assumed she had time to squander to one who now knows that no matter how many years her fate holds, there will not be enough.*[3]

The Kiss has received some harsh critical treatment because Harrison makes the erotic attraction between father and daughter mutual, and glides by the question of breaking cultural taboos by treating herself like the heroine in the fairy story—someone under a spell she can't resist. Stories of incest victims usually receive favorable treatment because the child is presented as the innocent object of someone else's illicit desire. It's Harrison's acknowledgment of mutuality that has shocked her critics—and made *The Kiss* a riveting story, albeit one which leaves many issues of the author's identity and familial relationships unresolved. The reader wonders whether she will ever be able to like other women, and thus like herself in later life, or whether she'll remain as exclusively focused on bonds with men as she was in her twenties.

In *The Shadow Man* (1996) Mary Gordon records her quest to find and understand the father who died when she was seven years old. Gordon is forty-six when she begins her research on her father's life. She's the proud worshiper of the memory of a man she thought went to Harvard, studied in the 1920s in Paris and at Oxford, was the racy editor of soft-porn magazines, was a Jewish convert to Roman Catholicism and became extremely right wing in the 1930s. Her father returned her adoration. A religious man, he once told her he loved her more than God. He taught her to read at three and made her memorize the Latin of the Mass at five.

When Gordon began her career as a writer, after Barnard College and graduate study at the University of Syracuse, she wrote novels about women who were utterly subservient to their fathers, and about the horrors of a rigidly Catholic upbringing. It wasn't until her forties that she began to wonder whether she could rely on the picture she'd cherished from childhood of the brilliant, eccentric man of faith who loved her. She'd always known that it was her mother who earned the family income, but as a child that hadn't seemed strange to her. Now, in midlife, it seems part of the larger puzzle of her identity.

Then there is the problem that the samples of her father's published writing that Gordon has kept from the past show a man who was obsessively anti-Semitic, a right-wing Catholic who thought well of Hitler and Mussolini. They also show a man whose sexual tastes were vulgar, a man who lived, on the rare occasions when he was working, on the fringes of the world of pornography.

This is the man who has made his daughter feel "special," lovable because so loved by him. She remembers the inscription on her copy of *A Child's Garden of Verses*.

My darling Mary Catherine, you have asked me to write you love letters in other languages, so here they are.

In German, French, Greek and Latin, my father was writing that he loved me. Now forty years later, my vanity, my sense of superiority over all living women, makes me pat my hair, stroke my cheeks, as if I've just been complimented on my beauty. Was there ever a little girl who was given anything like this? A girl who asked her father for love letters in different languages and got them?[4]

Here is the identity problem for a middle-aged woman intellectual. Her father published words, held ideas that make her feel that she has no right to love him in memory. That she should be denouncing him. Yet she wants to cling to the child she was, and the child's relationship to a doting parent.

I want to run into his arms, headlong, like the child who was the only one to know him as a father.[5]

But her final passage into adulthood requires that she face the past, and reconcile the contradictions between what her father wrote and what he was to his daughter.

Her search in the archives uncovers a startling story. Her father was born in Vilna, Russia, not Lorain, Ohio, as she had believed. He was given the name Israel, and his native language was Yiddish. He had a family of sisters—although he had always told her he was an only child. When she visited Lorain, Ohio, to learn about his schooling, she found that the family sold dry goods, lived over or behind the store. Instead of having gone to Harvard, he never finished high school. His first job at sixteen was as a clerk for the Baltimore and Ohio Railroad.

My father, my intellectual father. Not in the classrooms of George Lyman Kittredge, of Irving Babbitt, of Alfred North Whitehead, studying alongside T. S. Eliot and the nephew of Henry James. Nothing like that. He's an autodidact. Stealing time from his office job to read at the public library. . . . His writing makes sense in a wholly new way. The name-dropping.

The incoherence. The dream of the great, exalted, culturally embossed world.[6]

Next she finds that her father had abandoned his mother and sisters and allowed them to die as paupers in state or charitable institutions. Checks of passport records reveal that he never had a passport, so all his stories of study in Paris and Oxford were also pure fantasy. By this point there is little left of the man Gordon had lived with as a seven-year-old.

When she asks herself why she's destroyed her illusion, she isn't sure whether her search was an act of love or of vengeance.

Why was I digging in the archives? What was I looking for, and was my search in any way an act of love? Was it a vengeful act, like the uncovering of Noah by his drunken sons? Only worse, because it was done deliberately, scientifically? If I had loved my father above all things, would I have turned detective?[7]

She doesn't like the other searchers she sees in archives and libraries. They seem common to her—ill dressed, unlettered, sifting the past for lost kin and vanished connections. But she's finally humbled into realizing that she and they are engaged in one all-embracing task.

We are all trying to find a past that belongs to us. To assure ourselves that we are not alone. Thinking we can shed light on the darkness that was the world before our birth, that will be the world after our death.[8]

The reasons for Gordon's obsessive devotion to her father become clearer as her narrative unfolds the story of her mother. When Gordon undertook her quest to reconstruct the past, her mother was still alive but totally without memory. She was a woman crippled by childhood polio, always demanding help, always competent at work but an alcoholic at home with her solitary daughter. She was someone who could not give maternal care and affection—and someone so oblivious of the opinions of the rest of the world that she could live alone in a dirty, decaying house, so sodden with drink her daughter says she's "a blubbing, slobbering mess. A mess I had to clean up."[9]

Her relationship to both parents was brought to symbolic resolution when Gordon arranged a reburial of her father, in a plot that would bear his name, at a ceremony where his daughter and his grandchildren could be present. He'd been buried in her mother's family plot with no record of his name, no stone to mark his presence. Her memoryless mother was there for the ceremony, seeming to comprehend what was going on. For Gordon, reburying the man she had come know as her adult self laid the past of both her parents to rest and left her free to get on with her life.

Gordon is charting a major life transition in this narrative, an emotionally fraught event which lends excess to her language and makes her emphasize her childlike dependence for her sense of self in the present on a father who never was. It's hard to imagine a competent, middle-aged scholar made so distraught by dealing with her long dead father's past that her shaking hands can't thread film in a microfilm machine. Nor can we readily comprehend a married woman, with healthy and intelligent children, a loving husband and successful career who can assert that the most important fact about who she is is that her father died when she was seven. What she's telling us about is the life transition that enables her to live more fully in the present, having looked at her Jewish, Catholic, fascist father with the eyes of an adult scholar.

Harrison's and Gordon's examinations of father-daughter relationships are paralleled by three male narratives focused on traditional maternity as lived within impoverished and marginal families. *Angela's Ashes* (1997) by Frank McCourt (b. 1930) chronicles the life of his Irish mother, born in a Limerick slum, and his drunken Irish father, product of a farm in County Antrim. The story is one of unrelieved poverty, betrayal, the degradation of women and the exploitation of children, and yet, because McCourt has the narrative talent of a Dickens, it becomes a three-dimensional, richly detailed portrayal of a society, a way of life and an era that are unforgettable. McCourt's mother is the central character, the image of female endurance and oppression by men. She was a victim from the day of her birth, eventually corrupted by the grinding poverty she and her children endured. It was a grim childhood by any standard.

Nothing can compare with the Irish version: the poverty; the shiftless loquacious alcoholic father; the pious defeated mother moaning by the fire; pompous priests; bullying schoolmasters; the English and the terrible things they did to us for eight hundred long years.[10]

McCourt has a comic vision that enlivens the dreariest circumstances. He and his family have returned to Ireland from New York (where he was born), his father's drinking has left the family starving, his twin brothers and baby sister have died, yet he catches the humor of his two parents and their new charity false teeth in a memorable scene in their Limerick slum dwelling. The two were heavy smokers, even though there was never enough food. His mother had vowed to stop smoking when she got her new teeth—but somehow it didn't happen.

She says she'll give up the smoking when her new teeth are in but she never does. The new teeth rub on her gums and make them sore and the smoke of the Woodbines eases them. She and Dad sit by the fire when we have one and smoke their cigarettes and when they talk their teeth clack. They try to stop the clacking by moving their jaws back and forth but that only makes it worse and they curse the dentists and the people above in Dublin who made the teeth and while they curse they clack.[11]

McCourt watched the years go by—he was seven, eight, nine, ten—but still his father wasn't working, and his mother was trying to feed and house five people on the nineteen shillings and sixpence the family received as dole money. Whenever his father got a job, he lost it after the third Friday, because he drank his wages on the way home and missed Saturday work.

Yet McCourt loves his father. The noisy drunk didn't cancel out for his son the gentle father he was when sober. We hear the son's dilemma in the words of the child narrator.

I know when Dad does the bad thing. I know when he drinks the dole money and Mam is desperate and has to beg at the St. Vincent de Paul Society and ask for credit at Kathleen O'Connell's shop but I don't want to back away from him and

*run to Mam. How can I do that when I'm up with him early
every morning with the whole world asleep? He lights the fire
and makes tea and sings to himself or reads the paper to me in a
whisper that won't wake up the rest of the family. . . .*

*I think my father is like the Holy Trinity with three people
in him, the one in the morning with the paper, the one at night
with the stories and the prayers, and then the one who does the
bad thing and comes home with the smell of whiskey and wants
us to die for Ireland.*[12]

By the time McCourt was thirteen, his father had disappeared
in England, and when the family was evicted from their squalid
slum house for nonpayment of the rent, he saw his mother develop
a degrading relationship with the ugly and unkempt cousin who
gave them shelter. She became a slave to him and a not unwilling
sexual partner. When she complained about being ordered to per-
form humiliating menial services his response was "Woman's work,
Angela, woman's work and free rent."[13]

Eventually the cousin's treatment of Angela, and his malicious
taunting of McCourt, resulted in a fight in which McCourt was
badly beaten. He was appalled when his mother nonetheless settled in for the night with his tormentor. Feeling betrayed, McCourt
left the house and began to save for his passage to the United
States. The memoir closes with his arrival in Albany, and his de-
lighted recognition that he could enjoy life in his native country,
even though he would miss the extraordinary gallery of cousins,
aunts, friends, priests and drunks who are his Irish family.

By the time McCourt was fourteen, his father had disappeared
and his mother had failed him. He fulfilled all his private pledges
to support her and his brothers but remained unswerving in his determination to escape. In the course of the narrative, Angela, an
unequivocally maternal figure at its opening, has become someone
McCourt cannot trust, while his father remains the trinity of magical parent, friend and drunk. Gordon may have needed the
archives to help her comprehend her father, but McCourt has
gained his understanding a much harder way. *Angela's Ashes* may
cover his life only to the age of sixteen, but it contains a lifetime of
painful learning.

In *The Color of Water: A Black Man's Tribute to His White*

Mother (1996) James McBride (b. 1957) tells the story of his white mother and her black children. McBride is a lively narrator. A jazz saxophonist, composer and journalist, he began to tell his mother's story in an essay written for the *Boston Globe*'s 1981 Mother's Day issue. The piece attracted such an enthusiastic response that he embarked upon the memoir.

As the eighth of twelve children McBride doesn't remember ever being alone with his mother until the morning she took him to the bus for his first day at kindergarten. It wasn't until he was fourteen that he could get her to discuss her past with him—although he was bubbling with questions about this one white woman living happily with her mixed-race children in the tough Red Hook Housing Projects, surrounded entirely by black people.

He juxtaposes passages from her first-person account of her childhood and family with his own child's perception of his mother. In church, during a good, rip-roaring Baptist service, he'd watch his mother's tears flow and wonder about her.

> *Mommy's tears seemed to come from somewhere else, a place far away, a place inside her that she never let any of us children visit, and even as a boy I felt there was pain behind them. I thought it was because she wanted to be black like everyone else in church, because maybe God liked black people better, and one afternoon on the way home from church I asked her whether God was black or white.*[14]

She told him that God is no color, just the color of water, and that there's a world of the spirit where colors don't matter.

The sections of Ruth McBride Jordan's narrative explain why she was so determined to ignore race and religion. Born to an Orthodox Jewish family in Poland, she became child labor for her scheming father's store in Suffolk, Virginia, where he sold goods at 100 percent markup to the colored side of town. Her family life was miserable because her father mocked her mother's disability from childhood polio and carried on with other women. He also abused Rachel (Ruth McBride's birth name) sexually and bullied her mercilessly. The one happiness in her teenage life was an affair with a handsome young black neighbor, which became deadly dangerous for him when she learned she was pregnant. Her observant mother became her secret helper and arranged for her to visit relatives in New York, where she could secure the abortion that no one would discuss.

Right after her high school graduation, Rachel left for New York. Ready for adventure, she was even willing to play with the idea of becoming a prostitute. It was while she was being courted by an obvious pimp that Dennis McBride, a deeply Christian black friend, persuaded her she was making a mistake. When they began to live together, Rachel found herself respected and loved for the first time.

> *There was no turning back after my mother died. I stayed on the black side because that was the only place I could stay. The few problems I had with black folks were nothing compared to the grief white folks dished out. With whites it was no question. You weren't accepted with a black man and that was that. They'd say forget it. Are you crazy? A nigger and you? No way. They called you white trash. That's what they called me.*[15]

Rachel had wanted to see her mother during her last illness, but the family had no use for her. They'd sat shivah for her and regarded her as dead.

Yet, McBride remembers, she kept the Jewish passion for education and browbeat the New York City education authorities so that each of her twelve children went to predominantly white schools, in areas where most of their fellow students would be Jewish, and the Jewish love of learning would surround them. So their childhood was unlike that of most black children from Red Hook. Ruth McBride saw to it that it was different after school too.

> *The question of race was like the power of the moon in my house. It's what made the river flow, the ocean swell, and the tide rise, but it was a silent power, intractable, indomitable, indisputable, and thus completely ignorable. Mommy kept us at a frantic living pace that left no time for the problem. We thrived on thought, books, music and art, which she fed us instead of food.*[16]

In his twenties McBride was torn between being a musician and a journalist, which he saw as a choice between his blackness and whiteness. That uncertainty set him tracing his mother's family and learning about his Jewish heritage. It also made him search for all the traces of his minister father, who had died just before his birth. His father and mother were founders of the New Brown Memorial Baptist Church, one of the centers of hope in the Red Hook Housing Projects. Dennis McBride died of lung cancer at forty-five, but the family he'd established with Ruth went from strength to strength because she was so strong and so completely at home in her African-American world.

McBride had to write his and his mother's story because it was essential to understanding how to live the rest of his life.

> *The little ache I had known as a boy was no longer a little ache when I reached thirty. It was a giant, roaring, musical riff, screaming through my soul like a distorted rock guitar with the sound turned all the way up, telling me,* Get on with your life: Play sax, write books, compose music, do something, express yourself, who the hell are you anyway? *There were two worlds bursting inside me trying to get out. I had to find out more about who I was, and in order to find out who I was, I had to find out who my mother was.*[17]

McBride's drive to know his mother in order to sort out his own adult identity is very similar to Gordon's overwhelming need to know her father—but McBride had a living parent to interrogate. Both highly successful authors illustrate the craving to reconstruct a parent's life in order to negotiate the identity issue of their own adulthood. The giant riff screaming through McBride's soul tells us something about the difficulty of life transitions when directions are obscured by unusual patterns of race and religion, or by myths and silences about the past.

The celebration of his mother by Rick Bragg (b. 1959) is different. He knows who she is, all her kin, and all those of his no-good alcoholic father. He knows they are Southern poor whites, and that his world was kept in fragile continuity by the courage, self-denial and will to survive of his mother.

All Over but the Shoutin' (1997) is dedicated to Bragg's momma, Margaret Marie, born to a poor white family in the North Georgia mountains. Bragg depicts her as the archetypal suffering maternal figure, always willing to try again with the husband she loved even as he beat her brutally. She's the antithesis of a late-twentieth-century mainstream American woman—so self-abnegating she could be a character from a Victorian sentimental novel. She's also so unshakable in her will to survive for her children that she's like one of the stock redemptive figures in nineteenth-century American morality plays—the female savior in a temperance play like *The Drunkard*.

Her gifted journalist son wants to pay her honor, to give her the status and pride of place his father never did. For in the standard life plot of dirt-poor rural Georgia and Alabama, it's men who give women status. It is inconceivable that they could earn it for themselves.

The picture Bragg paints of his parents and the society in which they were so deeply rooted is loving, three-dimensional, a full-scale portrait in oils with a somber background derived from Bragg's rage at his father and ne'er-do-well younger brother, and his guilt that he got away to be a Pulitzer Prize–winning journalist at the *New York Times*, while his older brother, Sam, stayed trapped in poverty.

> *The biggest reason for writing this story is to set one thing straight from now on. My momma believes that she failed, that her three sons, being all she has ever had, did not get enough of the fine things in life because she was our mother. My older brother, Sam, has worked like a dog his whole life, in the coal yard and clay pits when he was eleven, with a pick and shovel and yard rake when he was a young man, and now in the cotton mill. If he has ever had a full day of rest in his life, I cannot remember when. She blames herself for that.*[18]

She also blames herself for her younger son's wild living and jail terms, but for Bragg, who was a Nieman fellow at Harvard in his early thirties, and a Pulitzer Prize winner at thirty-six, she takes no credit. But Bragg says he's inherited her backbone. She taught him, "Don't never take nothin' off nobody," and he hasn't. And, he says, "her sadness is in every story I write." He's chosen not to be a Washington correspondent, he's stayed telling stories about marginal people, and trying to capture their innate dignity, because that's what he learned from her.[19]

He's never reconciled to his father. On their last meeting, when his father was close to death from alcoholism and TB, Bragg waited for him to say he was sorry.

> *All I wanted was a simple acknowledgment that he was wrong, or at least too drunk to notice that he left his pretty wife and sons alone again and again, with no food, no money, no way to get any, short of begging, because when she tried to find work he yelled, screamed, refused. No, I didn't expect much.*[20]

By the time they were in their early teens, Rick and Sam had joined their mother in doing the toughest manual labor to earn a few pennies. Their mother picked cotton until the machine cotton picker arrived. Then she took in laundry. The boys did back-breaking kinds of rural labor.

> *The work was a hard and temporary thing that, I hoped, would pass in time. For me, it was a purification by fire, a thing that would make every other job, every other thing I ever did for the rest of my life, so laughingly easy by comparison.*
>
> *For Sam, it was the first step in a long, long walk, where the scenery seldom changed.*[21]

Even so the rules of the Southern class system began to loom large in Bragg's mind. After a few efforts at hiding his family background, Bragg learned to wear it like armor. If he brought home a girl who look horrified at the family dwelling and his mother's heaps of ironing, he never asked her out again. There were some who liked slumming, which was fortunate for him, because the only girls he was interested in were from above his station. The fires of ambition were beginning to burn, but the steely pride he took from his mother kept them in check.

Still, he slipped into the usual rural Southern ways in his last

years in high school—souped-up cars, days skipping school, parties
after ball games, no effort at study. He wasn't able to focus on lift-
ing himself out of poverty—just like everyone else in his world, he
lived for the moment. He thought it was luck when he was named
sports editor of the high school newspaper in his junior year. But
after graduation he was back doing construction work for an uncle
while everyone else was off to college.

Although he'd blown most of his savings on cars and girls,
Bragg had enough money left to enroll in one journalism class at
the local state college; then he volunteered for the college newspaper and covered sports. That led to a part-time job as a sports-
writer for the *Jacksonville News*. It was a new identity, flimsy at
first, but it took. He had dreams of moving to the nearby *Anniston
Star* but no hint of an idea that he was setting out on a path to the
New York Times and another world.

Once he'd made it to the *Times* he was lonely, and a little puzzled by the ambition that had carried him every step of the way
there. But it had also carried him away from his mother and
brother, and it was impossible for him any longer to explain to
them what he did. Sportswriting and his understanding of the
place of football in his native South had given him the chance to
leapfrog over the mistakes of his youth and the constraints of
poverty. His high school education was so poor he'd never have
made it into a good college or a strong journalism school, so it was
athletics and his passion for it that opened the way—though true
to his mother's upbringing, he likes to say God must have been on
his side.

His job put him to work beside Ivy League graduates, people
whose education and privilege intimidated him, so that, he says,
"the chip I had carried on my shoulder for a lifetime grew in those
years to about the size of a concrete block."[22] He kept telling himself the fates had given him extraordinary luck, getting him away
from poverty to working with all these highfalutin people. It was
easier to call it luck than to admit his talent, and his will to escape.

After successful assignments overseas and years reporting the
Florida scene, Bragg applied for a Harvard Nieman Fellowship.
Friends urged him to apply, he says, but he had to admit that Har-
vard and the Nieman Fellows Program "had something I wanted."
The something was validation of his intellect from a world of which

he'd always been secretly afraid. In his interview for the fellow-ship, much more was at stake than a year's education.

> *It was a test of whether or not I really belonged among these peo-ple, in this world, even if only for a year-long visit. Nothing they would tell me would make me feel less than proud of who I was or what I had done, over years. At least, I sure hoped not. No, this was a test of whether or not I could make them believe that I was smart enough to give something in return, something of value, to the finest university in the land. I had spent a lifetime telling myself I didn't give even a little bitty damn what the smart people thought. Yet here I was, hat in hand to them.*[23]

Of course he won a fellowship, and shortly afterward came the coveted *New York Times* job. When he passed muster at the *Times*, he was assigned to cover the South from Atlanta, and from there it wasn't a long journey to a Pulitzer Prize for feature writing.

> *This glorious thing, this prize, was validation of my mother's sacrifice. It was payment—not in full, but a payment none-theless—for her sweat, and her blood. "Now, people will speak to her when they see her on the street," explained one editor, a Southern man who knows something of snobbery, of class.*[24]

The way Bragg tells his story has many elements of the self-presentation common to women. The ambition never acknowl-edged, opportunities seized and improved upon put down to luck rather than talent. The sense of being an outsider in a profession where he feels he doesn't belong. His burning passion to right his mother's wrongs, force others to acknowledge her dignity and repay her for her lifetime of backbreaking labor is real, but it is also the cloak and shield for a level of ambition that might have been too dangerous for a Southern poor white male to hold, and it is the acceptable cover for the pains of leaving her behind. When the narrative ends Bragg has yet to establish real bonds with a woman of his own generation because he still sees women only in relation to their menfolk—one part of his heritage he hasn't been able to leave behind.

Mary Karr (b. 1954) and Bruce McCall (b. 1935) show us

another kind of childhood, lived within the circumference of compellingly dysfunctional families—Karr's a rip-roaring East Texas
childhood of gothic horror, McCall's an appropriately wry recollec-
tion of an Ontario boyhood. Karr's voice has the spellbinding
quality of Southern storytelling. McCall's understated humor
shows the irreverent joy in scrutinizing the ramshackle facade of
authority that makes Canada a country where the most popular
media show is the Royal Canadian Air Farce.

Karr has her own rich Dickensian power to evoke character
and patterns of speech so that her world of stern Protestants and
brawling, drunken oil workers comes alive on the page. This external world is juxtaposed with her childhood stream of consciousness, so that we see each dramatic scene in full Technicolor while
we listen to the child's inner commentary. The startling events described gain in piquancy from our consciousness of the child's effort to understand what's going on. Alongside the child's voice is
the adult Karr, commenting pithily on the events as she sees them
from adulthood.

> My mother didn't date, she married. At least that's what she said
> when I finally found out about all her marriages before Daddy.
> She racked up seven weddings in all, two to my father. My
> mother tended to blame the early marriages on her own mother's
> strict Methodist values, which didn't allow for premarital fool-
> ing around, of which she was fond.[25]

The Liars' Club is the group of drinking buddies with whom
Karr's working-class father played dominoes and told tall stories on
days off. Their language was colorful, filled with poetic imagery
and emphasized by a rich mosaic of swearwords. Her West Texas
maternal grandmother had a rich vocabulary also. Leechfield,
where the Karrs lived, was "a swamphole, a suckhole, and the anus
of the planet."[26]

The Karr household was wonderfully odd. Karr's parents had
an enormous bed, and the family took their meals sitting cross-
legged on the bed, leaning against one another's backs. The children bathed only when they felt like it, and, because of the heat,
they stripped down to underwear or pajamas whenever they were
indoors. The children never learned to respect their elders. Karr

would end her father's efforts at a whipping for bad behavior by shouting, "Go on and hit me then, if it makes you feel like a man to beat on a little girl like me."[27]

Karr's mother was known as "nervous," an East Texas euphemism for being given to bouts of insanity. And both parents drank heavily and fought bitterly, moving from verbal abuse to physical combat with their daughters as anguished witnesses. Karr and her older sister tried to make the battles funny by doing parodies of them and treating them as reels of a soap opera, but Karr's narrative conveys the deeper reality of the fear in which they lived. She says she couldn't tell

> *exactly what led to Mother's near-fatal attack of Nervous. Maybe drinking caused Mother to go crazy, or maybe the craziness was just sort of standing in line to happen and the drinking actually staved it off a while. All I know is that first Mother was drinking, then she and Daddy were fighting worse than ever, and finally they were hauling her away in leather four-point restraints.*[28]

The assumed toughness of her voice helps to emphasize the loneliness of the child observer who was watching her world fall apart. There are more scenes of madeness—Karr's mother getting ready to shoot her lover, Hector, and the children in the Colorado house she took after inheriting her mother's money and divorcing Karr's father. Karr had thrown herself across the body of her mother's lover, counting on her mother not to shoot her, no matter how ready she was to murder Hector.

> *A mist from somewhere inside her skull seemed to skitter behind her green eyes. She was considering. Her hand even dropped a few degrees from its straight-on angle. My poor babies, she said. Then the lines of her face drew up and hardened into something like resolve. Get offa him, Mary Marlene, she said. Hector's breath was wicked sour when he pleaded back to her, Honey . . . to which she said shut up.*[29]

The Karr children effected a rescue again, this time one for themselves. They called their father back in Texas and asked to come home. Not long after their mother returned, and the Karr ménage settled into its usual zany routines.

Karr escaped to college, tried to persuade her parents not to drink so much and to give up the cigarettes that were gradually suffocating her father with emphysema. All to no effect. It was on one of her journeys home after the stroke that came close to killing her father that she began to ask the questions that came out of her childhood, and to insist on answers. She had worked all the questions out with the help of a therapist, who kept on telling Karr she could live forever tormented by questions or insist on the answers. The answers were healing, because they made sense.

> *Nonetheless, truth was conspiring to assemble itself before me. Call it fate or grace or pure shithouse chance. I was being guided somehow into the chute that led down the dark corridor at the end of which truth's door would fly open.*[30]

Of course Karr, not fate, was the agent who opened Truth's door, even though she claims otherwise. What she saw was her mother's private tragedy. Her mother lost the children of her early marriage, stolen from her by a mother-in-law and husband who thought she was incapable of rearing them. She'd been on a steady journey down in the world ever since, settling on booze and tranquilizers to blot out the promise of the artist she once was. The story told, Karr and her sister could feel absolved of the long-held fear that they were the cause of their mother's madness, and their mother, her secret shared at last, could begin to get to know her daughters. So in Karr's closing chapter she and her family are moving beyond the storytelling of her father's Liars' Club into a clearer light of emotional truth. The blank fear of impending doom Karr had lived with since childhood is vanquished, replaced by a pattern of events that begins to make sense. The fates are still lurking in her last sentences, but they are showing signs of becoming benign. There's no way this story of needy children and wayward parents could have a happy ending, but acceptance and trust are good substitutes.

In *Thin Ice: Coming of Age in Canada* (1997), Bruce McCall tells the story of his childhood in Simcoe, Ontario. In the vignette that opens the narrative he's a solitary eleven-year-old, risking death by the side of Highway 3 in Southern Ontario, collecting matchbooks discarded from the cars of visiting Americans who are passing through Simcoe on the short Canadian route to the Midwest. McCall is from a line of Scots descended from a United Empire Loyalist, always eager participants in British wars and staunch defenders of Canadian culture against the rowdy, expansive American culture to the south.

But even at eleven, McCall wasn't so sure about the major dogma of Canadian culture—that everything American is inferior to everything Canadian. This feeling lurked even though Simcoe couldn't have seemed homier.

> *The eight-room North Public School was a ten minute walk . . . and its principal had taught our parents before us. The grade six teacher was our own Aunt May. A regulator clock, a portrait of King George VI, and a benevolent female person were fixtures of every classroom, and my classmates were my neighborhood chums.*[31]

This comfortable belonging was disrupted when McCall was twelve and a half by the family's move to Toronto, theoretically in search of happiness by uniting mother and children in the same house as the family breadwinner, who had been a commuter between Toronto and Simcoe for almost a decade. The move shattered beyond repair any illusion about a happy family. T. C. McCall disliked children and made no effort to disguise it. Peg McCall, a secret drinker during the years alone in Simcoe, settled for total inebriation by midafternoon, well before the children came home from school.

Both parents felt put upon by the size of their brood and, though long since unconcerned with one another, were united in disowning responsibility for the children.

> *A mother indifferent at best to the challenges of motherhood, a father carrying his fatherhood like a cross, the two united in a family raising policy based on resentment. Between them, in those little ways that even kids can't help but notice—avoiding physical contact, ensuring that requests for parental succor would get about what Oliver Twist's requests for more gruel got*

him—they soon enough managed to convey the unmistakable impression that we were being punished for ruining their lives.[32]

For McCall, growing up was a process in which his parents' absence was the major fact. When he was a child the absence was a puzzle. By late adolescence it was a source of anger verging on rage. Yet T. C. McCall could be wonderfully comic, could be tolerant of youthful mishaps and show the wit which made him a lively companion when with friends his own age. Peg McCall showed the quiet desperation of a woman whose life was no longer lit by dreams. Young and lively in her provincial town, she had married and become a young mother on the eve of the Great Depression. Codes of loyalty and faithfulness kept her in a loveless marriage, trapped in the wrong role with the wrong man. There was no circle of contemporaries with whom she could be another person, play a witty role, be admired, so her retreat into alcohol was complete.

This combination of parental characters meant that the younger McCalls suffered real neglect, amounting to abuse—their needs mocked and comfort for childhood ills deliberately withheld. Their older siblings knew it but did nothing.

There was one effort by the older children to penetrate their mother's sodden world. The three older boys settled on decisive action, only to sink deeper into the psychic ailments of a deeply depressed woman.

It is late one November night in 1949 in the living room at 2337 Danforth. T. C. is away on another business trip. Mother is drunk again. . . . Mike, Hugh and I are stewing in our bedroom when Mike decides to break the McCall taboo against direct encounters and get to the root of mother's addiction, once and for all. Why, why, why this suicidal slide into alcoholism? What is so wrong with her life? Isn't there some way to help, to stop her from continuing to inflict this misery on herself and her family?[33]

The response, completely untrue, is that she took to drink because she was dying of cancer—but *no one must know. It must never be mentioned to T. C.* This gratuitous brutality left her three older sons watching with fear and anguish for the signs of her mortal illness. When they didn't appear, the boys slowly concluded that they'd been had.

In this suffocating emotional environment, with no possibility of release, McCall was forced to live a life of the imagination, cramped into the handkerchief-sized bedroom he shared with an older brother. The room became a pressure cooker for the creative life. McCall sees the outcome as accidental—but for the pressure cooker to deliver more than steam required talent.

> *But from this accident of circumstance, this small-scale improvised working example of necessity as the mother of invention, I would extract first a diversion, then a hobby, then a calling and ultimately a professional career. A rotten start. I don't know where I would be today without it.* [34]

McCall actually experienced the early deaths of both parents (when they were forty-nine) as a liberation. Their departure was the essential ingredient for his newfound sense of agency. He no longer ascribed success to fortune, but to his own energy and drive. He had some frustrating years as a commercial artist, but his life moved onto a smooth and enjoyable track when he found a job at the publishing house of McLean-Hunter. He might have been a lowly copyboy, had holes in his shoes that let in the Toronto winter slush, but as the new trainee in McLean-Hunter's Editorial Services he was a dynamo of energy.

> *It was Editorial Services' good fortune to be providing typewriter and paper to a just-burst dam of writing energy, and my inconceivable good fortune to be actually encouraged to vent a pent-up lifelong urge. I couldn't write enough. . . .*
>
> *Nothing in life had come as easily to me as writing. Coming on McLean-Hunter was coming home. To feel in my natural element after those fumbling, stumbling, half-assed years of futility in commercial art changed how life itself felt. I was no longer grimly hanging on, dragged wherever destiny chose to take me; I was in command. I was good at something, and because I was, I could hold up my head and look the world in the face.* [35]

Writing took him across the border, and eventually to his literary home at *The New Yorker*. Living in the United States, free from mother country and the stuffy imperial attitudes his unnurturing parents had exemplified, he felt the magnetic pull of being "near the center of things." That continental force stirred more energy within him and made him acknowledge ambition. His gifts made the rest happen. But being Canadian by birth, he still needed to underplay what happened. He lived on Central Park West, was married and was *somebody*.

> *I let a childish vision, a self-created fairy tale, be my guide. And damned if it didn't work.* [36]

If we look at this crop of memoirs as a group, some of the fairy-tale quality attaches to every one of them. Folk stories are built upon archetypal perceptions of inadequate nurturing, on the fear of evil parents or siblings, on the good brother or kind grandparent who rescues the situation—on the helpful fate or destiny that reassures that the world is not hostile. It's not surprising that these elemental themes should appear in memoirs by young writers, and it is a sign of the times that we are responding with such riveted attention to tales of needy children. So the primal feelings drive these bleak narratives as surely as they do the tales of the Brothers Grimm.

The story of the inadequate family surely must become one of the central cultural themes of the late twentieth century, since almost 50 percent of children experience family breakup. What undergirds the male celebrations of heroic or suffering mothers is the conservative political idealization of the traditional female— pregnant, suffering, the victim of wicked men, the unswerving, undeviating lover, but never rival, of her son. Certainly Frank Mc-Court's Angela is an ambiguous figure, but she exhibits the traits of the quintessential Victorian female victim.

Harrison's and Gordon's fathers have to be characterized as inadequate to outright evil. Gordon sees the evil in her father's strident fascism—but wants to retain her sense of the good in the man—something she can do only in a fictional section of *Shadow Man*, entitled "Seeing Past the Evidence," where she puts her father—and those she thinks made him what he was in reaction to virulent American anti-Semitism—on trial. It's the section of the book that works least well because it leaves the Holocaust to one side and weakens the evil of the ideas through the flawed character of Gordon's father.

Harrison's father, as depicted surely among the seedier Protestant clerics in American literature, is shown with little perspective on his character except the acknowledgment of his missionary parents, and of his anger at being dragooned by a powerful mother to become a preacher. It makes him hate women, his clerical garb, the mother church and, it seems, everything female but his daughter's body. He gets a special kick out of having sex with his daughter in his office at the church. He seems demonic, and Harrison is no Mary Karr, wanting to know why. Both memoirs can be seen as unraveling some of the moral and intellectual pretenses which shore up patriarchy, but both also convey the primal emotions of the fairy tale, except that instead of a punishing superego we see a postmodern consciousness at work trying to analyze the plot.

McBride, Karr and McCall are busy dismantling the myths which have swirled about their incomprehensible and chaotic family lives. McBride and Karr are intent on letting in the light of truth, at least as they see it, while McCall disposes of absent parents by absenting himself from their country, and abandoning curiosity about his origins. There is no giant riff in his soul about the family past because he believes he's discarded the myth his parents' identity rested upon and remade himself as an American—a remaking easier for the blankness of the earlier family, a problem McBride and Karr surely do not have.

CHAPTER NINE

WORD AND IMAGE

Until we lose it we take memory for granted. Along with language it is the force that makes us human. It gives us the cultural context for the miraculous power of communication. Memory was Mnemosyne for the Greeks and Minerva with her owl for the Romans—a powerful goddess with a beneficent face. We need to cultivate her, because it matters how we remember things.

If we remember the past as a series of chaotic events governed by an impersonal and nonmoral fate or luck, we create a similar kind of future in our mind's eye, and that prophecy is usually self-fulfilling. If we see the past as fully determined—by economic forces, by genetic codes, even by birth order and relationship to parents—we see ourselves as victims of those forces, with our best hope a kind of stoic resignation. If we see our past as a moral and spiritual journey in time, our imagined future will continue that quest. We might not use the imagery of Dame Julian of Norwich, but we'll be in the same existential position as she was—pondering the intersection of our tiny point of human consciousness with the metaphysical pattern she called the mind of God.

We travel through life guided by an inner life plot—part the creation of family, part the internalization of broader social norms, part the function of our imaginations and our own capacity for insight into ourselves, part from our groping to understand the universe in which the planet we inhabit is a speck. When we speak about our memories, we do so through literary forms that seem to capture universals in human experience—the quest, the romance, the odyssey, the tragic or the comic mode. Yet we are all unique, and so are our stories. We should pay close attention to our stories. Polish their imagery. Find their positive rather than their negative form. Search for the ways we experience life differently from the inherited version and edit the plot accordingly, keeping our eyes on the philosophical implications of the changes we make. Was this action free? Was that one determined? How does the intersection of the two change the trajectory of a life?

I recall as a young college student listening with astonishment to a lecture laying out the 1950s social science orthodoxy about the psychology of women and the accompanying patterns of life which gave them fulfillment. They were supposed to be concerned only with the expressive, managers of emotion, governed by a biological destiny. "But that's not my experience!" I said, rejecting out of hand the notion of female passivity and lack of intellectual drive. Much of my young adulthood was spent reconstructing that then widely accepted view of what a woman's life was all about. I recall even earlier in life, perhaps age seven sitting on my swing—a homemade affair, suspended from a eucalyptus tree, in decent privacy, far away from the house on my parents' Australian sheep station—wondering out loud how I was going to get away from this isolated place to somewhere near great events and important ideas I read about in the newspapers and heard on the radio. At seven I was already at work on planning a life story different from the one that went with rural Australia. Most of us begin that process of editing by interrogating the past. What can we make of our parents, grandparents, the network of kin who constitute our tribal past? If we can know them, they are a set of compass points by which we can chart our own course. If we can't know them, James McBride's powerful riff in the soul becomes urgent, as many recent memoirs show. But what exactly is the process of questioning the past?

We know a little more about Minerva and the ways she speaks to us these days because the sciences that study the brain keep uncovering more fine detail about how memory works. We know that the brain takes in experience as word and image, but that there is also an uncharted territory in the brain, where experience is stored in a form called, for lack of a better term, the nonverbal or preconceptual. Through the technology of imaging electronic events in the body, we can see memory being searched—watch the delicate tracery of networks flickering, see the brightly lit nodes of activity in different areas of the brain that signify where word and image are being melded together to constitute what we are conscious of as memory. But it is in the sequencing and interpretation of the information we recall that the forms and tropes of culture take effect. And it is the examination and interrogation of that sequencing and interpretation that constitute the craft of the autobiographer. It was this interaction between word, image and cultural form that excited Freud and Jung, and led them to develop techniques for analyzing their patients' relationships to past events. They did so with interpretive theories shaped by the biases and unexamined assumptions of their time, but the intersection point between culture and the stored traces of past experience is *the* most revelatory point for understanding the tension between individual and society. It is the place we have to look to understand the assertion that some human quality or mentality is "socially" or "culturally" determined.

We all practice the craft of autobiography in our inner conversations with ourselves about the meaning of our experience, and those conversations, no matter what language we use, are fundamentally theological or philosophical. Though only a handful of us set about writing down the results and publishing them for others to read, we are all autobiographers. But few of us give close attention to the forms and tropes of the culture through which we report ourselves to ourselves. Though they capture universals in human existence, these forms are not necessarily the perfect expressions of our experience in our unique passages through time. So we should be wary of the psychological traps inherent in inherited modes of expression.

Take the romance for example. The romantic heroine is someone acted upon, someone who responds to others, someone who is not the agent of her own destiny. Yet in reality we all make choices and manipulate others, though it is not part of the romantic life plot for the heroine to acknowledge what she's done. But agency unacknowledged even by the actor in question means a power for action not subject to moral constraints. Western culture has elevated the romantic heroine to a preeminent place in its governing myths, and, at least until very recently, has regarded women as less morally developed than men, or less able to exercise abstract moral reasoning. But it's hard for someone who doesn't acknowledge agency, even to herself, to reason very cogently about the morality of her actions. Once we've acquiesced in concealing our agency from ourselves and others, we've lost our moral moorings.

We can spot the moments when we are slipping into this mode of thinking, whenever our inner life plots find expression in the passive voice, or whenever chance or destiny is in charge of the action, because that grammatical mode or that notion of causation means we've so construed our lives that we can't subject our actions to moral scrutiny. Converting the active to the passive voice and ascribing the causal force in life to luck or destiny was once a particular snare for women, but it is just as much a problem for men at the margins of society—for whom acknowledgment of their ambitions may be dangerous. Whatever our biological sex, we should be wary of seeing our stories as romances because using that form will encourage us to confuse the nature of causation in our lives.

Then there is the related myth of the maternal female, always nurturant, always able to process everyone else's emotions, the caregiver who is at her best when those around her are in crisis. Then she can take center stage, in charge in every disaster. This maternal female is the inspiration for many strands of contemporary feminism, from the ecofeminist movement, whose adherents see women as the caregivers of the planet, to lesbian separatist groups, who want to base a worldview on women's connectedness to others. But there is something profoundly unattractive about needing others to be down or in crisis in order to be one's best self. The caregiver needs to be needed, often so badly she'll help create the need—like the mothers who invent illnesses for their children so they can gratify their obsession with the role of all-provident, caring female. Making the caregiver female also encourages men to overlook the ways others care for them, and allows them to underestimate the need to nurture others in whatever organizations they find themselves.

The odyssey has its traps for the would-be Odysseus who can't call upon helpful gods and goddesses to deal with the demons in his life and whose agency, no matter how impressive, cannot influence the impersonal operations of forces, like world markets, or natural disasters, like hurricanes and earthquakes. And despite endless evidence to the contrary, young men, and very recently young women, keep on believing that the experience of warfare will be heroic along classical Greek lines. Then there are the misguided warriors we see every day, whose occupations call for the arts of peace and negotiation but who know only the call of battle.

A variant of the odyssey is the life plot of the romantic rebel, intent on dismantling cultural forms which have become archaic or are politically outmoded. This is a role played by both men and women, and one in which the rebellion becomes a life-consuming force, seeming to subsume all other activity. But there is actually no transfer from rebellion against one kind of authority to authority in other areas of one's life. So we see Martin Duberman, romantic radical historian, still unquestioning about the authority of psychiatrists, or Gloria Steinem, full-time feminist leader, slipping into the role of caregiver for the feminist movement and unable to care for herself.

Rebellious anger at past betrayals still doesn't convey the voice to speak on one's own behalf, as we see in the women and working-class male writers who set out to tell a parent's story into which they slip as much of their own as they can. But cultivation of that voice—the power of speaking for oneself—is a prerequisite for maturity, because until we've found our own voices we can't settle down to ask ourselves and others probing questions about life in the present. In a long life as a feminist, the question I have been asked most frequently is "How do you make yourself heard?" as if being listened to was a matter of volume or tone of voice. We're heard when we speak confidently out of our understanding of our own experience. One can talk about that quite softly and still be listened to. It is the derivative or the unexamined experience others screen out. Of course Western society has socialized women to report only derivative experience, say what will make people feel good rather than what they really think—so the problem of one's participation in discourse being registered by others is seen as a gendered one, though many working-class or minority males have the same experience.

Two recent memoirs may serve to illustrate these generalizations. In *Personal History* (1997) Katharine Graham (b. 1917), publisher of the *Washington Post* and the most commanding wielder of Washington power and influence of her generation, tells the story of her life as though personal ambition and the exercise of power were utterly alien to her temperament.[1] Trained to see her life as a romance, she apparently did not resent her father's decision to turn over the controlling ownership of the *Post* to her husband, Philip Graham, nor did she ask herself, or anyone else, penetrating questions about Philip Graham's erratic behavior, until events reached a point of crisis and it was no longer possible to ignore his manic-depressive condition. By that time her husband was infatuated with another woman and was planning to divorce Graham and take complete control of the newspaper empire which was the creation of her father.

Once her husband's condition was diagnosed, Graham surrendered authority over his treatment to psychiatrists and, as she tells it, simply exercised no personal judgment about whether the treatment was effective. So when Philip Graham, immensely persuasive in a manic phase, wanted to get out of the hospital and come to their country house for the weekend, she didn't question going off there alone with him to a house well-equipped with every kind of hunting rifle.

Philip Graham's suicide and Katharine Graham's ensuing battle to seize control of the *Post* again fit the stereotypical romantic story, because the classic heroine is allowed to show strength when left without a partner—society loves the "plucky widow." However, what is riveting about Graham's story is her gradual development into the powerful woman who decided to publish the Pentagon Papers, although half her senior advisers argued against it. It was Graham's decision to back the investigative reporting team who uncovered the Watergate scandal, and it was Graham who learned corporate finance in order to manage relations with major shareholders better once the *Post* became a public company.

Clearly she is a woman capable of trenchant analysis and decisive action, but her memoir shows that she was very slow to recognize these qualities in herself, and that even as the publisher of the *Post* she still felt as though she were a hesitant, inexperienced housewife. She had a problem with voice, especially in her inner conversations with herself—a problem which lasted long after she'd found her voice in public. The evidence in the story she is telling so powerfully points to the emergence of the strong public self that the reader becomes a little impatient with Graham's inability to recognize what she has become. But the inability is real, and it's Graham's sense that the story of her life has to do with her relationship to a husband that keeps getting in the way of a clearer perception. We are hearing a story from a woman who can't relate self to action, and who feels that the power of action conferred by her widowhood and her wealth is somehow not rightly hers. This is a cautionary tale because if a woman who creates her own destiny as surely as Graham has can't really experience that she's doing that, there is little hope for others.

By contrast, Jean-Dominique Bauby (1952–1997), a French journalist felled at forty-three by a stroke that left him in paralysis except for the capacity to see out of and blink his left eye, managed to retain a sense of agency even though condemned to a life of total reliance on others. He might well have seen himself as a victim—since his stroke left him afflicted by what is called locked-in syndrome, a consciousness shut in a body which allows it no action. He learned to communicate by blinking his left eye at the letter he wanted to use as someone read the alphabet to him. By that means he composed *The Diving Bell and the Butterfly* (1997), a memoir of his experience living beyond the stroke. His shut-in state, a mind functioning within a body without power of motion, was like being held in a diving bell. But the flights he could take in mind and imagination made him see himself as a butterfly, a common symbol for the soul. On those flights he was constantly giving orders and making plans.

> *For now, I would be the happiest of men if I could just swallow the overflow of saliva that endlessly floods my mouth. Even before first light, I am already practicing sliding my tongue toward the rear of my palate in order to provoke a swallowing reaction. What is more, I have dedicated to my larynx the little packets of incense hanging on the wall, amulets brought back from Japan by pious globe-trotting friends. Just one of the stones in the thanksgiving monument erected by my circle of friends during their wanderings. In every corner of the world, the most*

*diverse deities have been solicited in my name. I try to organize
all this spiritual energy. If they tell me that candles have been
burned for my sake in a Breton chapel, or that a mantra has
been chanted in a Nepalese temple, I at once give each of the
spirits invoked a precise task.* [2]

Here was a man with as strong a sense of agency as St. Augustine, and as big a drive to improve the moment as Benjamin
Franklin, and he was capable of keeping on doing that despite the
trauma of learning that he was literally a mind shut in his body.

When the first autumn came after his stroke, Bauby recognized it as the first one in which he wouldn't be bustling back to
work after summer vacation. The rest of the world may have been
intent on settling down to new tasks; his task was one from which
there was no vacation—to learn to live with his condition and comprehend its meaning. In the closing pages of *The Diving Bell and
the Butterfly*, Bauby describes watching the woman who has been
his scribe as she reads out the text which her painstaking counting
of his blinks has produced. His gaze falls on the articles she has
spread out around her.

*I will put them in my mind's scrapbook as reminders of a sum-
mer of hard work. The big blue notebook whose pages she fills
with her neat, formal handwriting; the pencil case like the ones
schoolchildren use, full of spare ballpoints; the heap of paper
napkins ready for my worst coughing-and-spitting fits; and the
red raffia purse in which she periodically rummages for coins for
the coffee machine. Her purse is half open, and I see a hotel
room key, a metro ticket, and a hundred-franc note folded in
four, like objects brought back by a space probe sent to earth to
study how earthlings live, travel, and trade with one another.
The sight leaves me pensive and confused. Does the cosmos contain keys for opening up my diving bell? A subway line with no
terminus? A currency strong enough to buy my freedom back?
We must keep looking. I'll be off now.* [3]

Bauby's sense of agency makes him see himself as in charge
even in so dire a predicament. And as a result his way of looking
at his life situation is primarily moral and metaphysical. There is

a richness and texture in the valuation he places on life which makes the neediness and demanding tone of a narrative like *The Kiss* sound thin and its author's perspective on life seem narrow. Of course, the aspects of life experience now appearing in autobiography would once have been addressed only in fiction—since the social taboos on discussing incest, family violence and other kinds of abuse were censors of what should appear in autobiography. So today we read these youthful memoirs as stories in which the line between fiction and autobiography is even less distinct than in the past.

Yet when they work well these youthful memoirs tell us the value of connecting with the past in some profound fashion. In my family the large, unanswered question governing my generation's understanding of the past was about the manner of my father's death, when he was fifty-four and I was ten. Did he intend to drown himself in the dam on the family property, or was his death the result of a stroke or heart attack? It makes a difference, even fifty years later, whether his going was intentional or not.

Recently my brother unearthed his medical records deep in the recesses of the Australian war archives—medical records kept up to date to the day of his death fifty-three years ago because he received a disability pension for wounds incurred in the fighting around Passchendaele in the 1914–1918 War. They told me something very important. He and I have the same pattern of heart fibrillations—there they were, recorded on the grainy paper of fading army medical forms—the same pulse rate, the same blood pressure, the same unexplained onset. That connection in the genes is a new way of looking at a chain of being of which he and I are intimate parts. Here's a visible sign of the genetic material that lives on in me. I used to look upon my sudden fibrillations as a nuisance, an intrusion on the day's plans, an interruption in a closely scheduled life, an encroachment on a tightly bounded ego. Now when they begin I'm aware of the continuity and more likely to smile and say, "Well, Dad. How shall we play this one?" Those forms also tell me that his departure from life at such an early age was most likely involuntary—a piece of knowledge which changes the emotional and moral climate of my childhood, a personal evidence of how much history matters.

Notes

CHAPTER ONE

1. St. Augustine, *Confessions,* trans. with an introduction by Henry Chadwick (New York: Oxford University Press, 1991).

2. Jean-Jacques Rousseau, *The Confessions,* with an introduction by J. M. Cohen (New York: Viking Penguin, 1953), bk. 1.

3. Bernal Díaz del Castillo, *The Discovery and Conquest of Mexico (1517–1521).*

4. Malcolm X, *The Autobiography of Malcolm X,* with Alex Haley (1966); James Baldwin, *Giovanni's Room* (1953) and *The Fire Next Time* (1966); Jawaharlal Nehru, *Toward Freedom* (Boston: Beacon Press, 1958); Mohammed Ali Jinnah, *Collected Works* (Karachi, Pakistan: East and West Publishing, 1984); James Merrill, *A Different Person* (New York: Alfred A. Knopf, 1993).

5. Hildegard of Bingen, *Scivias,* trans. C. Hart and T. Bishop (New York: Paulist Press, 1990), 14, 26. A shortened version (ed. Fiona Bowie and Oliver Davies; trans. Robert Carver) appears in *Hildegard of Bingen: An Anthology* (London: SPCK, 1990).

6. *The Shewings of Julian of Norwich,* ed. Georgia Ronan Crampton (Kalamazoo: Medieval Institute Publications, Western Michigan University, 1993), 77.

7. *The Life of St. Teresa of Avila, By Herself,* trans. J. M. Cohen (1957), most readily available in Penguin Classics.

CHAPTER TWO

1. Jean-Jacques Rousseau, *Confessions,* trans. with an introduction by J. M. Cohen (New York: Viking Penguin, 1953), 23.

2. *The Autobiography of Benjamin*

Franklin, intro. by R. Jackson Wilson (New York: Modern Library, Random House, 1981), 19.

3. Franklin, *Autobiography,* 112.
4. Franklin, *Autobiography,* 35.
5. Franklin, *Autobiography,* 152.
6. Rousseau, *Confessions,* 386.
7. *Life and Times of Frederick Douglass written by himself* (New York: Pathway Press, 1941), 96.
8. Douglass, *Life and Times,* 158–59.
9. Douglass, *Life and Times,* 381.
10. Andrew Carnegie, *Autobiography of Andrew Carnegie* (New York: Doubleday, 1920).
11. Henry Ford in collaboration with Samuel Crowther, *My Life and Work* (Garden City, N.Y.: Doubleday, Page, 1922), 64.
12. Ford, *My Life,* 3.
13. Ford, *My Life,* 35.
14. Ford, *My Life,* 50.
15. Ford, *My Life,* 264.
16. W. E. B. Du Bois, *The Autobiography of W. E. B. Du Bois: A Soliloquy on Viewing My Life from the Last Decade of Its First Century* (New York: International Publishers, 1968), 192.
17. Du Bois, *Autobiography,* 197.
18. Du Bois, *Autobiography,* 214.
19. Du Bois, *Autobiography,* 281.
20. Du Bois, *Autobiography,* 305–6.
21. Du Bois, *Autobiography,* 395.
22. Lee Iacocca with William Novak, *Iacocca: An Autobiography* (New York: Bantam Books, 1984), 31.
23. Iacocca, *Iacocca,* 54.
24. Iacocca, *Iacocca,* 131.
25. Iacocca, *Iacocca,* 149.
26. James D. Watson, *The Double Helix: A Personal Account of the Discovery of the Structure of DNA* (New York: Atheneum, 1968), 37.
27. Watson, *Double Helix,* 128.

CHAPTER THREE

1. Mary Rowlandson, *The Sovereignty and Goodness of God, Together with the Faithfulness of His Promises Displayed,* in *Held Captive by Indians: Selected Narratives,* ed. Richard VanDerBeets (Knoxville: University of Tennessee Press, 1973), 53.
2. *A True Relation of the Birth, Breeding, and Life, of Margaret Cavendish, Duchess of Newcastle, Written By Herself,* critical preface by Egerton Brydges (Kent: Johnson and Warwick, 1814), 308.
3. Rachel Plummer, *Narrative of the Capture and Subsequent Sufferings of Mrs. Rachel Plummer, Written by Herself,* in VanDerBeets, *Held Captive by Indians,* 353.
4. Anna Cora Mowatt, *Autobiography of an Actress, or Eight Years on the Stage* (Boston: Ticknor and Fields, 1854), 132.
5. Mowatt, *Autobiography,* 132–3.
6. Harriet Ann Jacobs, *Incidents in the Life of a Slave Girl* (Boston, 1861). Facsimile edition in Classic Slave Narratives series, ed. with an introduction by Henry Louis Gates Jr. (New York: Mentor Books, 1987), 426.
7. Jacobs, *Incidents,* 513.
8. Jane Addams, *Twenty Years at*

Hull-House (New York: Macmillan, 1910), 85.

9. Addams, *Twenty Years,* 67.
10. Addams, *Twenty Years,* 276–77.
11. Margaret Sanger, *Margaret Sanger: An Autobiography* (New York: W. W. Norton, 1938), 86–87.
12. Sanger, *Autobiography,* 91.
13. Sanger, *Autobiography,* 92.
14. Ellen Glasgow, *The Woman Within: An Autobiography* (Charlottesville: University Press of Virginia, 1994), 153.
15. Glasgow, *Woman Within,* 154–55.
16. Glasgow, *Woman Within,* 296.
17. Glasgow, *Woman Within,* 160.
18. Gloria Steinem, "Ruth's Song (Because She Could Not Sing It)," in *Outrageous Acts and Everyday Rebellions* (New York: Holt, Rinehart and Winston, 1983).
19. Vivian Gornick, *Fierce Attachments: A Memoir* (New York: Simon and Schuster, 1987), 22–24.
20. Gornick, *Fierce Attachments,* 76–77.
21. Gornick, *Fierce Attachments,* 78.
22. Gornick, *Fierce Attachments,* 203.

CHAPTER FOUR

1. David Livingstone, *Livingstone's Private Journals, 1851–1853,* ed. with an introduction by I. Schapera (Berkeley: University of California Press, 1960), 16, 132.
2. Livingstone, *Private Journals,* 132.
3. Livingstone, *Private Journals,* 38.

4. Livingstone, *Private Journals,* 25.
5. Emily C. Judson, *Memoir of Sarah Hall Boardman Judson of the American Mission to Burmah* (New York: Sheldon and Co., 1872), 149.
6. Judson, *Memoir,* 158.
7. Judson, *Memoir,* 167.
8. Henry M. Stanley, *The Autobiography of Sir Henry M. Stanley,* ed. Dorothy Stanley (Boston: Houghton Mifflin, 1909), 327.
9. Stanley, *Autobiography,* 330.
10. Richard Burton, *First Footsteps in East Africa, or, An Exploration of Harrar,* vol. 1 (London: Tylston and Edwards, 1894), 206–7.
11. Burton, *Harrar,* 208–9.
12. Burton, *Harrar,* 81–82.
13. Mary Kingsley, *Cheltenham Ladies College Magazine,* no. 38 (Autumn 1898), quoted in Stephen Gwynn, *The Life of Mary Kingsley* (London: Macmillan, 1933).
14. Mary H. Kingsley, *Travels in West Africa, Congo-Français, Corisco and Cameroons* (London: Virago Press, 1982), 87.
15. Kingsley, *Travels,* 89.
16. Kingsley, *Travels,* 248.
17. Kingsley, *Travels,* 273.
18. Kingsley, *Travels,* 608.
19. Kingsley, *Travels,* 545.
20. Gertrude Lowthian Bell, *Syria: The Desert and the Sown* (New York: E. P. Dutton, 1907), 1.
21. Bell, *Syria,* ix.
22. Bell, *Syria,* ix.
23. Bell, *Syria,* 1–2.
24. Bell, *Syria,* 60.
25. Bell, *Syria,* 249–50.

26. T. E. Lawrence, *The Seven Pillars of Wisdom* (Garden City, N.Y.: Doubleday, Doran, 1935).

27. Siegfried Sassoon, *Memoirs of an Infantry Officer* (New York: Coward McCann, 1930), 85.

28. Sassoon, *Memoirs,* 87.

29. Sassoon, *Memoirs,* 112–15.

30. Sassoon, *Memoirs,* 231.

31. Peter Ryan, *Fear Drive My Feet* (Carlton: Melbourne University Press, 1985), 3.

32. Ryan, *Fear Drive My Feet,* 133.

33. Ryan, *Fear Drive My Feet,* 233.

34. Ryan, *Fear Drive My Feet,* 251.

35. Ryan, *Fear Drive My Feet,* 3.

36. Vera Brittain, *Testament of Youth: An Autobiographical Study of the Years 1900–1925* (New York: Macmillan, 1934), 341.

37. Brittain, *Testament,* 342.

38. Brittain, *Testament,* 411, 418–19.

39. Winnie Smith, *American Daughter Gone to War: On the Frontlines with an Army Nurse in Vietnam* (New York: William Morrow, 1992), 60.

40. Smith, *American Daughter,* 119.

41. Smith, *American Daughter,* 237.

42. Smith, *American Daughter,* 322.

CHAPTER FIVE

1. Harriet Martineau, *Autobiography,* vol. 1 (London: Virago Press, 1983), 41.

2. Martineau, *Autobiography,* 42.

3. Martineau, *Autobiography,* 142.

4. Martineau, *Autobiography,* 180.

5. Martineau, *Autobiography,* 248.

6. Martineau, *Autobiography,* 180.

7. Martineau, *Autobiography,* 260.

8. Elizabeth Cady Stanton, *Eighty Years and More* (1898). This memoir appears as volume 1 of *Elizabeth Cady Stanton As Revealed in Her Letters, Diary and Reminiscences,* ed. Theodore Stanton and Harriet Stanton Blatch (New York: Harper and Bros., 1922).

9. Stanton, *Eighty Years,* 69.

10. James G. Birney was an anti-slavery candidate for the presidency and a member of the conservative Abolition group. Stanton, *Eighty Years,* 69.

11. Stanton, *Eighty Years,* 145.

12. Stanton, *Eighty Years,* 150.

13. Stanton, *Eighty Years,* 154.

14. Stanton, *Eighty Years,* 155.

15. Stanton, *Eighty Years,* 155.

16. Stanton, *Eighty Years,* 174.

17. Stanton, *Eighty Years,* 160–61.

18. Stanton, *Eighty Years,* 211.

19. Stanton, *Eighty Years,* 273.

20. Stanton, *Eighty Years,* 305.

21. Emmeline Pankhurst, *My Own Story* (London: Eveleigh and Nash, 1914).

22. See Susan Kingsley Kent, *Sex and Suffrage in Great Britain, 1860–1914* (Princeton, N.J.: Princeton University Press, 1987).

23. Pankhurst, *My Own Story,* 59, 12.

24. Pankhurst, *My Own Story,* 43.

25. Pankhurst, *My Own Story,* 48.

26. Pankhurst, *My Own Story,* 56.

27. Pankhurst, *My Own Story,* 255.

28. Pankhurst, *My Own Story,* 323.

29. Addams to Mary Linn, April 1, 1889, Addams Correspondence, Swarthmore

College Peace Collection, Swarthmore, Pa.

30. Jane Addams, *Twenty Years at Hull-House* (New York: Macmillan, 1910).

CHAPTER SIX

1. Virginia Woolf, "Reminiscences," in *Moments of Being: Unpublished Autobiographical Writings,* ed. with an introduction and notes by Jeanne Schulkind (Sussex: University Press, 1976), 55–56.
2. Woolf, "Reminiscences," 58.
3. Woolf, "A Sketch of the Past," in *Moments of Being,* 68–69.
4. Woolf, "Sketch of the Past," 124.
5. Woolf, "Sketch of the Past," 126.
6. Woolf, "22 Hyde Park Gate," in *Moments of Being,* 142–55.
7. Woolf, "22 Hyde Park Gate," 154–55.
8. Mabel Dodge Luhan, *Intimate Memories:* vol. 1, *Background* (New York: Harcourt, 1933); vol. 2, *European Experience* (New York: Harcourt, 1935); vol. 3, *Movers and Shakers* (New York; Harcourt, 1936); vol. 4, *Edge of Taos Desert: An Escape to Reality* (New York: Harcourt, 1937).
9. Luhan, *Background,* 223.
10. Luhan, *Background,* 223.
11. Luhan, *Background,* 250.
12. Luhan, *Movers and Shakers,* 188.
13. Luhan, *Movers and Shakers,* 242.
14. Luhan, *Movers and Shakers,* 482.
15. Luhan, *Edge of Taos,* 36.

16. Germaine Greer, *Daddy, We Hardly Knew You* (New York: Alfred A. Knopf, 1989), 45.
17. Greer, *Daddy,* 50.
18. Greer, *Daddy,* 67.
19. Greer, *Daddy,* 70.
20. Greer, *Daddy,* 84.
21. Greer, *Daddy,* 152.
22. Greer, *Daddy,* 308.
23. Gloria Steinem, "Ruth's Song (Because She Could Not Sing It)," in *Outrageous Acts and Everyday Rebellions* (New York: Holt, Rinehart and Winston, 1983), 143.
24. Gloria Steinem, "Doing Sixty," in *Moving Beyond Words* (New York: Simon and Schuster, 1994), 249.
25. Steinem, "Doing Sixty," 258.
26. Gloria Steinem, *Revolution from Within* (New York: Little, Brown, 1992).
27. Steinem, "Doing Sixty," 259.

CHAPTER SEVEN

1. May Sarton, *Plant Dreaming Deep* (New York: W. W. Norton, 1968), 23.
2. Sarton, *Plant Dreaming Deep,* 25; Margot Peters, *May Sarton: A Biography* (New York: Alfred A. Knopf, 1997), 150–53.
3. Sarton, *Plant Dreaming Deep,* 180.
4. Kate Millett, *Flying* (New York: Alfred A. Knopf, 1974), 15.
5. Millett, *Flying,* 75.
6. Millett, *Flying,* 143.
7. Millett, *Flying,* 22.
8. See Carolyn Heilbrun's thoughtful analysis of these events in her life of Gloria Steinem, *The Education of a Woman* (New York: Bantam

Doubleday Dell, 1995), 164–68.

9. Audre Lorde, *Zami, A New Spelling of My Name* (Watertown, MA: Persephone Press, 1982), 7.

10. Lorde, *Zami,* 139.

11. Lorde, *Zami,* 160.

12. Lorde, *Zami,* 179.

13. Lorde, *Zami,* 255.

14. Martin Duberman, *Cures: A Gay Man's Odyssey* (New York: E. P. Dutton, 1991), 20.

15. Duberman, *Cures,* 39.

16. Duberman, *Cures,* 68.

17. Duberman, *Cures,* 63.

18. James Merrill, *A Different Person* (New York: Alfred A. Knopf, 1993), 192.

19. Merrill, *Different Person,* 90.

20. Merrill, *Different Person,* 38.

21. Merrill, *Different Person,* 42.

22. Merrill, *Different Person,* 43.

23. Merrill, *Different Person,* 203.

24. Merrill, *Different Person,* 244–45.

25. Jan Morris, *Conundrum* (New York: Harcourt Brace Jovanovich, 1974), 103, 170.

26. Morris, *Conundrum,* 14.

27. Morris, *Conundrum,* 79.

28. Morris, *Conundrum,* 25.

29. Morris, *Conundrum,* 106.

30. Morris, *Conundrum,* 149.

31. Jan Morris, *Pleasures of a Tangled Life* (New York: Random House, 1989), 11.

CHAPTER EIGHT

1. Kathryn Harrison, *The Kiss: A Memoir* (New York: Random House, 1997), 63.

2. Harrison, *Kiss,* 70.

3. Harrison, *Kiss,* 190.

4. Mary Gordon, *The Shadow Man: A Memoir* (New York: Random House, 1996), 48.

5. Gordon, *Shadow Man,* 104.

6. Gordon, *Shadow Man,* 127.

7. Gordon, *Shadow Man,* 160.

8. Gordon, *Shadow Man,* 163.

9. Gordon, *Shadow Man,* 238.

10. Frank McCourt, *Angela's Ashes: A Memoir* (New York: Charles Scribner's Sons, 1997), 11.

11. McCourt, *Angela's Ashes,* 139.

12. McCourt, *Angela's Ashes,* 210.

13. McCourt, *Angela's Ashes,* 281.

14. James McBride, *The Color of Water: A Black Man's Tribute to His White Mother* (New York: Riverhead Books, 1996), 50.

15. McBride, *Color of Water,* 232.

16. McBride, *Color of Water,* 94.

17. McBride, *Color of Water,* 266.

18. Rick Bragg, *All Over but the Shoutin'* (New York: Pantheon Books, 1997), xix.

19. Bragg, *All Over,* xx.

20. Bragg, *All Over,* 12.

21. Bragg, *All Over,* 103.

22. Bragg, *All Over,* 141.

23. Bragg, *All Over,* 218.

24. Bragg, *All Over,* 296.

25. Mary Karr, *The Liars' Club: A Memoir* (New York: Viking Penguin, 1995), 10.

26. Karr, *Liars' Club,* 33.

27. Karr, *Liars' Club,* 45.

28. Karr, *Liars' Club,* 125.

29. Karr, *Liars' Club,* 253.

30. Karr, *Liars' Club,* 311.

31. Bruce McCall, *Thin Ice: Coming of Age in Canada* (New York: Random House, 1997), 16.

32. McCall, *Thin Ice,* 24.

33. McCall, *Thin Ice,* 101.

34. McCall, *Thin Ice,* 118.

35. McCall, *Thin Ice,* 223.

36. McCall, *Thin Ice,* 249.

CHAPTER NINE

1. Katharine Graham, *Personal History* (New York: Alfred A. Knopf, 1997).

2. Jean-Dominique Bauby, *The Diving Bell and the Butterfly,* trans. Jeremy Leggatt (New York: Alfred A. Knopf, 1997), 12–13.

3. Bauby, *Diving Bell,* 131–32.

BIBLIOGRAPHICAL NOTE

The critical and theoretical literature on autobiography is vast. To consult a subject index in any library under the heading "Memoirs" today is to see that since the early 1950s, when theorists first became interested in autobiography as a genre, there has been an almost exponential growth in writing on the subject.

In the 1950s, '60s and '70s the focus of attention was on whether autobiography was a genre in its own right, or just a defective form of fiction. In the 1980s new forms of literary analysis—deconstructionist and poststructuralist—changed the way we view texts and analyze narrative. Developments in linguistics changed the way we look at metaphor and symbol, and the field of cultural criticism led us to discourse analysis, and a new set of questions about why some experiences are included in "literature" and other experiences are left out of the conversation entirely. If these intersecting trends forcing revision of how we see storytelling caused one kind of interpretive crisis, there has been, since the late 1970s, an equally profound theoretical and critical shift in the way feminist scholars assess women's autobiography and understand its reception, so that feminist questions have required new readings of narrative by and about women.

The works listed here will help the interested reader begin to enter into this lively literature. The choices are idiosyncratic. They are the works I have found most helpful, but another student of the genre might well suggest ten other equally interesting ways to engage the subject.

James Olney's *Metaphors of the Self: The Meaning of Autobiography* (Princeton, N.J.: Princeton University Press, 1972) is a helpful introduction to the subject, stressing the male process of identity formation. His volume *Autobiography: Essays Theoretical and Critical* (Princeton, N.J.: Princeton University Press, 1980) contains a translation of Georges Gusdorf's famous 1956 essay "Conditions and Limits of Autobiography," in which Gusdorf, professor emeritus of philosophy at the University of Strasbourg, focused attention on autobiography as something more than a bastard kind of fiction. *Studies in Autobiography,* edited by Olney and published by Oxford University Press in 1988, captures the work of an international conference on autobiography held at Louisiana State University in 1985. Its focus was the history, theory and critical response to the genre, now acknowledged as a mode in its own right. In this symposium Georges Gusdorf's essay "Scripture of the Self, Prologue in Heaven" characterized the autobiographical mode as "the knowing of knowing, where subject and object overlap each other." William Spengemann's *Forms of Autobiography: Episodes in the History of a Literary Genre* (New Haven: Yale University Press, 1980) offers the best historical perspective on the subject, with a seventy-five-page bibliographical essay on the rapidly growing field. And Philippe Lejeune's study of memoir and autobiography, *On Autobiography,* edited and with a foreword by John Paul Eakin, translated by Katherine Leary (Minneapolis: University of Minnesota Press, 1989), introduces the notion of the authorial pact between narrator and reader, an idea which has persisted in critical response to the genre. John Sturrock's *The Language of Autobiography: Studies in the First Person Singular* (New York: Cambridge University Press, 1993) brings the linguistic issues in autobiography into focus. Mark Freeman, in *Rewriting the Self: History, Memory, Narrative* (London: Routledge, 1993), draws on concepts from history, psychology, philosophy and literary theory to analyze the process of self-reporting and the insights it offers on developmental transitions. He does so in language that is free from jargon and easily comprehensible to the nonspecialist reader.

Women's Autobiography: Essays in Criticism, edited by Estelle C. Jelinek (Bloomington: Indiana University Press, 1980), is an essential introduction to women's relationship to the genre. *The Private Self: Theory and Practice in Women's Autobiographical Writing,* edited by Shari Benstock (Chapel Hill: University of North Carolina Press, 1988), is a useful survey of the theoretical issues raised by women's self-narratives. Helen M. Buss's *Mapping Ourselves: Canadian Women's Autobiography in English* (Montreal and Kingston: McGill–Queens University Press, 1993) opens with an essay which reviews the standard theories about how a male identity is formed and indicates the ways theorists concerned with women's autobiography are changing or modifying male models of identity formation. Buss writes with admirably simple prose about a subject encrusted with abstruse technical language, so her opening chapter is useful to any reader concerned with women's autobiography. Her reading of great Canadian women's memoirs is striking for its originality, and her approach is easily transposed to other historical experiences.

Terry Eagleton's *Literary Theory: An Introduction* (Minneapolis: University of Minnesota Press, 1996) is the most recent edition of his lucid introduction to a complex subject. Eagleton wants to make literary theory comprehensible to a wide body of readers, and he has succeeded. Anyone can read this book with benefit, and all readers can use it to pose and answer literary questions for themselves.

Taken as a whole, this body of writing about autobiography suggests some of the creative new directions emerging in the humanities. The earliest writing about deconstruction, poststructuralism and discourse analysis was nearly impenetrable to the nonspecialist, and the authors seemed more concerned with technique than with meaning. Freeman and Buss seem to me fine examples of a new and expansive humanism freed from the class and elitist aspect of earlier literary studies but every bit as concerned with the ways we understand human experience as Homer, Thucydides, Dante or Dame Julian of Norwich.

Some of the themes developed in this volume have been of little past interest to general readers, or have been so recently developed that they have not yet been incorporated in a larger cultural setting. Here are some easily available entry points into further reading about them.

June Namias, a valued colleague at M.I.T., first set me reading captivity narratives. Her *White Captives: Gender and Ethnicity on the American Frontier* (Chapel Hill: University of North Carolina Press, 1995) was a first attempt at analyzing styles of reporting the experience of being taken hostage by Indians, and her commentary on this subject has illuminated many other captivity texts for me.

Sarah Boardman Judson's extraordinary life can best be understood through Joan Jacobs Brumberg's *Mission for Life: The Judson Family and American Evangelical Culture* (New York: New York University Press, 1984). Marion Tinling's *Women into the Unknown: A Source Book on Women Explorers and Travellers* (New York: Greenwood Press, 1989) is a great introduction to a fascinating subject. The extraordinary body of memoirs produced by women who served in Vietnam can be tapped through Deborah A. Butler's *American Women Writers on Vietnam: Unheard Voices, A Selected Annotated Bibliography* (New York: Garland Publishing, 1990). *American Nurses in Vietnam: The Forgotten Veterans,* edited by Dan Freedman (Austin: Texas Monthly Press, 1987), captures the experience which was so devastating for a generation of American nurses.

There is still no really compelling biography of Elizabeth Cady Stanton. Lois Banner, in her *Elizabeth Cady Stanton: A Radical for Women's Rights* (Boston: Little, Brown, 1980), and Elizabeth Griffith, in *In Her Own Right: The Life of Elizabeth Cady Stanton* (New York: Oxford University Press, 1984), do their best to unravel the life of this complex woman, but there's more work to be done before we get this story as straight as history and narrative allow.

There is also no good biography of Emmeline Pankhurst, though Susan Kingsley Kent's *Sex and Suffrage in Britain, 1860–1914* (Princeton, N.J.: Princeton University Press, 1987) makes the dynamic of the suffrage battle unfold as if according to a rational plan, whereas earlier writers have tried to explain Mrs. Pankhurst away as an untrustworthy radical or a sentimental utopian whose policies were a series of ad hoc actions.

Quentin Bell's biography of his famous relative, *Virginia Woolf, A Biography* (New York: Harcourt Brace Jovanovich, 1972), was long the authoritative source on the life of Woolf, but Hermione Lee's *Virginia Woolf* (New York: Alfred A. Knopf, 1997) provides a welcome fresh perspective on Woolf's life. No satisfactory biography exists of Mabel Dodge Luhan, despite the extraordinary detail in which she documented her version of her life. Lois Palkin Rudnick, in *Mabel Dodge Luhan: New Woman, New Worlds* (Albuquerque: University of New Mexico Press, 1984) and Winifred L. Frazer, in *Mabel Dodge Luhan* (Boston: Twayne Publishers, 1984), provide useful biographical information but little context into which to place Luhan's remarkable life.

INDEX

Jill Ker Conway was born in Hillston, New South Wales, Australia, graduated from the University of Sydney in 1958, and received her Ph.D. from Harvard University in 1969. From 1964 to 1975 she taught at the University of Toronto and was vice president there before serving for ten years as president of Smith College. Since 1985 she has been a visiting scholar and professor in M.I.T.'s Program in Science, Technology, and Society. She now lives in Boston.

She is the author of *Merchants and Merinos* (1960), *The Female Experience in Eighteenth- and Nineteenth-Century America* (1982), *Women Reformers and American Culture* (1987), *The Road from Coorain* (1989), and *True North* (1994) and editor of *Written by Herself: Autobiographies of American Women* (1992) and *Written by Herself, Vol. 2: Women's Memoirs from Britain, Africa, Asia, and the United States* (1996). She has also edited (with Susan C. Bourque and Joan W. Scott) *Learning About Women* (1989) and (with Susan C. Bourque) *The Politics of Women's Education* (1993).

A NOTE ON THE TYPE

This book was set in Fairfield, the first typeface from the hand of the distinguished American artist and engraver Rudolph Ruzicka (1883–1978). In its structure Fairfield displays the sober and sane qualities of the master craftsman whose talent has long been dedicated to clarity. It is this trait that accounts for the trim grace and vigor, the spirited design and sensitive balance, of this original typeface.

Rudolph Ruzicka was born in Bohemia and came to America in 1894. He set up his own shop, devoted to wood engraving and printing, in New York in 1913 after a varied career working as a wood engraver, in photoengraving and banknote printing plants, and as an art director and freelance artist. He designed and illustrated many books, and was the creator of a considerable list of individual prints—wood engravings, line engravings on copper, and aquatints.

Composed by Creative Graphics, Allentown, Pennsylvania
Printed and bound by R. R. Donnelley & Sons,
Harrisonburg, Virginia
Designed by Robert C. Olsson